Art,
Economics
and
Change

The Kulebele of Northern Ivory Coast

Dolores Richter

PSYCH/GRAPHIC PUBLISHERS

LA JOLLA, CALIFORNIA

Book Design: Patricia L. Bessell
Editorial Consultant: Dawn S. Rawls
Photographs: Dolores Richter

ISBN: 0-932382-01-0
Library of Congress Catalog Card Number 79-90941

For my grandfather R. M. Richter
and my sons Craig and Keith

Contents

Motivations of the African Artist: Religious and/or Economic? — The Tourist Art Market: An Innovation? — Tourist Art Market Participation as a Source of Social Change — Definitions of Terms.

Fijembele — Kulebele History and Demography.

Kinship — Marriage — The *Kacolo* — Impact of Inheritance and Housing Laws — Men's and Women's Roles.

Political Organization — Poro Age Grades — Poro as an Instrument of Political and Economic Manipulation — Political Organization and Islam.

Maps

Tables

Diagrams

Plates

Preface

This book is a re-written version of a dissertation written for the Department of Anthropology, Southern Illinois University, Carbondale. The fieldwork upon which it is based was carried out in Ivory Coast from July 1973 to December 1975. I established residence in a Kulebele concession in Korhogo in October 1973 and remained there until December 1974. In April 1975 I moved to be close to a Fonombele concession, but contact was maintained with Kulebele and visits were made to them several times a week until October 1975. Numerous visits of one to several days each were made to rural Kulebele settlements and host-villages in the eastern area. Two weeks and several shorter visits were spent on the north-south axis of Ouezoumon to San investigating western Kulebele and corroborating data gathered in Korhogo from western Kulebele in residence there.

Data were collected by participant observation and indirect and direct questioning. Open and closed questions were used as well as schedules concerned with voluntary work groups, patron-client relationships, residence patterns, capital investments and prestige spending. Kinship and migration genealogies were gathered and censuses taken. Oral tradition was collected from Kulebele and oral tradition concerning Kulebele and attitudes toward Kulebele were collected from Senufo and *fijembele*. Government publications, newspapers and archival material were searched for historical background and pertinent data. African and European dealers in tourist and traditional art objects were interviewed in Korhogo and Abidjan and their storerooms visited. Shops selling art objects in Abidjan were visited to establish fixed retail prices and the distribution of Kulebele carvings. Photography was used to record voluntary work groups, social groups, patron-sponsored work groups, residence patterns, carving techniques and carved objects for the purpose of comparison.

The fieldwork was conducted primarily in French which is spoken by many young Kulebele men. A working knowledge of Senari was helpful in checking data and attitudes concerning subjects discussed in French with the researcher. An English-speaking Guleo, who also speaks French and three Senari dialects, provided valuable assistance in translating conversations and oral texts.

The research upon which this book is based was supported by the National Science Foundation, the National Institute of Health and Southern Illinois University grants from the College of Liberal Arts, the Graduate School and the Department of Anthropology. I am very grateful for their having made my work possible.

I would like to thank all those who encouraged and helped me during the course of my fieldwork and the preparation of the manuscripts that ultimately became my dissertation and this book. Dr. William Welmers very kindly provided me with my first lesson in Senari. Dr. Philip J. C. Dark, my dissertation chairman, and Dr. M. Lionel Bender were never-ending sources of intellectual guidance and moral support. Dr. Nelson H. H. Graburn made many helpful suggestions, Dr. Wade C. Pendleton was a constant source of encouragement and Ms. Marjorie Burke very helpfully translated German sources for me and made many helpful editorial suggestions. I also want to thank Pat Bessell for her enthusiasm and encouragement during the preparation of this book.

Many people in Ivory Coast extended help and hospitality in order that I could pursue my studies. Dr. Georges Nyangoran-Bouey, Director of the Institut d'Ethno-Sociologie at the Université d'Abidjan, and his colleague, Mr. Moriba Touré, were extremely helpful in expediting the formalities required for doing fieldwork in Ivory Coast. Mr. Banga Koné very kindly introduced me to the Kulebele community in Abidjan which led to my being welcomed by Kulebele in Korhogo. Mr. and Mrs. Albert Votaw generously opened their home to me during my visits to Abidjan for which I am most grateful. Especially kind were Mr. and Mrs. Jean-Francois Boggio whose generous hospitality in Korhogo afforded welcomed relief from the rigors of fieldwork. I should also like to thank Miss Melba Means for her hospitality.

It is not possible to mention all the Kulebele who helped make my research more rewarding and fruitful. Specifically, however, I should like to mention Fobé Coulibaly, chief of the Korhogo

Kulebele, who allowed this stranger to settle among his people, and El Haj Kassoum Coulibaly, who acted as my *jatugu* during my stay with the Kulebele and who provided a home and hearth for me when I first arrived in Korhogo. With particular affection I wish to thank Ngolo Coulibaly from Bolpe and Ngolo Coulibaly from Kolia for their interest in my work and for their patience with my ignorance of things Kulebele. They were kind and patient teachers. Finally, I must not forget Souleymane Coulibaly, my buddy and my Guleo *piu*.

A Note on Orthography

All the Senari words in the text are Dalir which is the Senari dialect spoken by eastern Kulebele. Senari is a tonal language but tones are not indicated in the text. Neither is nazalization which is a prominent feature of Dalir. I have avoided using Senari words in the text where an English word will suffice. When Senari words do occur in the text the following orthography is used:

a as in f*a*ther
e as in b*e*t
i as in f*i*t
o as in b*o*w
ɔ as in *ought*
u as in t*oo*
c as in ca*tch*
j as in fu*dge*
r is always flapped
7 is a glottal stop

The International Phonetic Alphabet is used on kinship diagrams.

The orthography for proper nouns follows the French. The names of towns and villages are taken from maps NC-30-VII Korhogo (1963), NC-29-XII Boundiali (1964), NC-30-XIII Niéllé (1954) and NC-29-XVII Tengrila (1964) published by the Institut Géographique National, Paris. Spellings on these maps sometimes vary slightly from those used on Michelin map 172 (1973) of Ivory Coast, but they generally agree with official roadsigns.

Two Senari words used in the text, Poro (a type of secret society) and *sinzang* (sacred grove), have no plural forms.

Introduction

One often comes away from reading about African art with the impression that the African artist is a noble savage who has been corrupted by Western contact; that the source of the artist's inspiration has been uprooted by the deterioration of his religious beliefs; that he has been seduced and corrupted by Western currency, and that the impersonal nature of the tourist art market has adulterated his esthetic goals. But as pertinent questions are asked another picture of the artist, his craft and his market emerges: participation in the tourist art market is a means for introducing changes in social organization, accommodating pressures due to modernization and evolving new esthetic cannons.

The monograph which follows investigates the extent of these changes in a specific case, woodcarvers of the northern Ivory Coast. A study is made of the Kulebele way of life and the changes that have occurred in their social organization in response to external forces such as Islam, enhanced economic opportunity and state programs aimed at modernization. The tourist art market influences modern Kulebele life in elaborate and interdependent ways, but to study effectively this influence we must ask first about the artist's previous patterns of motivation and the development of the tourist art market.

Motivations of the African Artist: Religious and/or Economic?

The literature concerning African art has traditionally stressed the mystical and religious motivations of the African artist. The "creative impulse," writes von Sydow (1928:225), "was intimately concerned" with "religious and social institutions, such as secret societies, ancestor worship, belief in gods, or initiation rites. . ." Beinart (1965:8) states that changes in these institutions "have left the religious artist with no inspired purpose . . . no

1

creative framework. . ."[1] There have been, however, dissenting voices. Crowley (1972:25) states that "A great deal of nonsense has been written about the supposed insoluble relationship between African traditional religion and art."[2] Herskovits (1967:434-435) has also objected to the mystical emphasis: "The culture-bound discussions of African art never took the human element into account. The ways in which the African artist produced his masterpieces were rarely if ever mentioned. . . . Presumably the African artist produced his masterpieces solely because of some archetypal urge. . ." Fagg (1961:466) points out that "The economics of carving are of great importance in any study bearing on the survival value of tribal art. . ."

A careful examination of the literature reveals the economic aspect of African craftsmen although, in most cases, the relationship between financial rewards and the motivation to be a craftsman is not dealt with. Duke, writing in the eighteenth century, notes that he paid a blacksmith ". . . one rod, five Booster yams, and one jar of mimbo. . ." for putting copper leg bracelets on a lady friend (Forde 1968:62). Forde and Scott (1946:136 and 188) and Nadel (1969:264-288) are precise about what Nigerian artisans are paid. Other writers note the financial rewards realized by craftsmen but are less precise: Bangway carvers "earn their living" from their carving activities (Brain and Pollock 1971:39); Zulu blacksmiths received goats for their work (Ritter 1973:46); skilled Anang carvers are able to accumulate considerable wealth and prestige (Messenger 1973:103); and a Kran carver notes the many woman he "bought" and distributed among his sons and nephews with earnings realized from carving (Himmelheber 1963:97).[3] That payment to craftsmen requires sacrifice on the part of the customers is noted by Bravmann (1974:161fn) and Glaze (1976:112), all of which suggest that more than mystical inspiration motivates the African artist.

Crowley (1973:249) makes a useful distinction between "professional artists" and "nonprofessionals working under the inspiration of religion." He describes professionalism as being a degree of specialization (ibid:233). Professionals consider themselves, and are considered by others, primarily as being craftsmen who realize a large part, or all, of their livelihood from their craftsmanship. They are paid for their work and are often accustomed to working for a wide variety of customers, many of whom may not be members of the craftsman's own ethnic group and may not share a religious iconography or belief system.

Examples of professional artisans working for out-groups are noted in Himmelheber who mentions Baule artists who work for Agni kings (1972:191) and itinerant Kran carvers who work for groups hostile to the Kran (1963:96-97). Ibo blacksmiths are also itinerant and work for a variety of groups other than their own (Cole 1972:85; Forde and Scott 1946:214; Neaher 1976:96-97). While itinerant craftsmen may be cognizant of the iconography and religious beliefs of their foreign patrons, it seems doubtful that their creative inspiration would be stimulated by a commitment to the religious beliefs of strangers. Indeed, as we shall see, a lack of understanding of the iconography and symbolism of a patron's religious beliefs need not hamper a professional master craftsman. While pleasure of creation and praise from patrons may be important rewards for the professional artist, the fact remains that he earns much of his living from his work.

The Tourist Art Market: An Innovation?

Because being paid for one's production and working for out-groups are not unfamiliar to professional artists, the step from working for traditional purposes to working for the Western art market is not such a great one. The artist's purpose is essentially the same—to earn a living, acquire wealth and gain prestige. However, social scientists have attempted to differentiate between the traditional market and the tourist art market. Herskovits (1967:435 and 439) notes that the development of the tourist art market created a situation in which the African craftsman ". . .began to produce for a clientele he did not know." Bascom (1976:313) writes of tourist art market producers: "The artist's ultimate customers are not merely strangers; they are foreigners, not even members of his own ethnic group." The tourist art market, then, is an impersonal market in which there is no interaction between producer and consumer. Another difference noted in the literature is production in anticipation of sales rather than working on commission which is believed to be traditional (Bascom 1976:313; Herskovits 1967:440). A third difference is mass-production which is mentioned within the context of tourist art market production (Bascom 1976:321; Goldwater 1964:119; Herskovits 1967:436-437; May 1974:2), but is not discussed within the context of traditional production.

However, mass-production in anticipation of sales for an impersonal market has long been present in the traditional marketing of weaving, brasscasting, leather work, blacksmithing, pottery and woodcarving in West Africa. Boahen (1968:298-303) reports trans-Saharan caravans as early as the seventeenth century originating in northern Nigeria that included cloth and leather goods made for export in Kano and Nupe. H. Barth (1965:Vol. III) called Kano a "manufacturing town" in 1857 where large quantities of cloth, ready-made men's clothing and leather sandals were produced for export to other parts of West Africa and to North Africa. Barth, Caillié (1968:Vol. I) and Clapperton (1826:53) all describe a large variety of African-made items for sale in local markets in the nineteenth century, such as wool blankets, natural and dyed cloth, ready-made clothing, leather items, mats, pottery, wooden bowls, iron blooms, scissors and knives, copper drinking vessels, brass bells and jewelry, and glass, coral and amber beads, which were both of local manufacture and imported from other African towns and villages. A 1928 French administrative report (Rapport 1928) notes quantities of brass rings and cloth among the goods transported by caravans from Ivory Coast to the Niger. Glaze (1976:338) mentions brass charms and divining paraphernalia for sale in indigenous markets in Ivory Coast where I have also seen substantial stocks of brass, aluminum, iron, leather and wood charms and divining paraphernalia, cloths, pottery, baskets, mats, and iron, wood and leather utilitarian items manufactured in large quantities, for unspecified consumers and in anticipation of sales.[4] Granted that major ritual items such as face and helmet masks and most statutary are executed on commission and involve personal encounters between consumer and craftsman, nonetheless, the concept of production in anticipation of sales to unknown consumers is not an alien concept in West Africa.

Tourist Art Market Participation as a Source of Social Change

Schädler (1976) has stated that tourism has little affect on traditional values or arts and crafts and that changes that do occur in these areas are the result of the abandonment of traditional religious beliefs. However, Barth (1967), Durstan (1970) and Hammond (1970) make it clear that new economic opportunities can result in the adjustment of traditional values and social organization. Tourism and the tourist art market present new economic opportunities which, as Foster (1967:305) found, can be a fragmenting influence on traditional institutions and a source of social change.

Innovators are often agents of change. Foster (ibid:293) writes that innovators are ". . . a basic key to understanding change." Indeed, the title of a book on social change by Barnett is *Innovation: The Basis of Culture Change.* Foster (ibid:304) states that innovators are motivated by the desire for economic profit and new forms of prestige. But are tourist art market producers innovators? It has been pointed out above that the characteristics associated with the tourist art market, e.g., mass-production in anticipation of sales to unknown consumers, are not unfamiliar in West Africa and that although new kinds of wares have been introduced for the tourist market, the marketing processes are the same as those implemented in the traditional market. The brasscaster who mass-produced charms and jewelry but cast ritual masks only on commission in the past has simply added to his inventory of items to be sold to unspecified consumers when he casts masks in anticipation of sales in the tourist art market.

However, tourist art market craftsmen are subject to experiences different from those of traditional craftsmen. Rather than being part-time specialists, as is often the case among traditional artists,[5] they are full-time specialists who are able to support themselves and their families with their tourist art market earnings.[6] As full-time specialists they are not involved in subsistence activities such as farming and the cooperative relationships often associated with farming as are part-time craftsmen. Tourist art market producers work for cash, whereas traditional craftsmen often receive food and livestock for their work (Maduro 1976:241; Williams 1976:381). The tourist craftsman, then, is committed to a cash economy, whereas the traditional craftsman is often involved in a subsistence economy. Further, the tourist craftsman usually earns more for a week's or a month's work than the traditional craftsman, which earnings may be invested in traditional ways of gaining prestige such as title-taking, acquiring wives and attracting dependents, or spent on European goods, modernizing one's house, investing in income-producing ventures such as a truck or rental property, or educating children.

Because of the potential for income, people are attracted to the business of producing for the tourist art market. In the traditional setting, many of them would not have found a market for their wares because of lack of expertise in their *métier* as will be shown in the pages that follow or, perhaps, because their production has no place in the traditional setting. This is paticularly true of carvers, though other artistic mediums have also been developed especially for tourist art market consumption.[7] Examples of a new genre of carvers are to be found throughout the world: Mexico (Ryerson 1976), northern Japan (Low 1976), New Guinea (Abramson 1970), Canada (Graburn 1976b) and, of course, Africa (d'Azevedo 1970:52; Ben-Amos 1976; Shore-Bos 1969; Stout 1966).

The tourist art market may also provide the means by which Fourth World artists are able to cope with social changes resulting from external contact.[8] Graburn (1976a:45-47) describes how Canadian Eskimos were able to realize new wants that developed as a result of Canadian development in their area by carving for the tourist art market. Williams (1976:266) states: "The marketing of arts produced by Aborigines at Yirrkala has been an important factor in the transition from a hunting-and-gathering economy to a cash-based economy." Ryerson (1976:127) notes a similar phenomenon occurring with the Seri Indians in northern Mexico as does Stromberg (1976:150-151) with the bark-paper painters in Xatitla, Mexico. Thus, earnings realized from tourist art market participation may be disruptive of tradition, but they may also be the means of responding to new and potentially disruptive contacts.

Another area in which the tourist art market may impinge upon the traditional is concerned with style, motif and technique of traditional arts. The traditional artist conforms to the stylistic conventions and motifs embraced and understood by his clients and which are familiar to him. Indeed, often the iconographic features on ritual pieces are dictated by the customer, not the craftsman. I do not intend to imply that traditional art is rigid and unchanging, for it is not, as Bascom (1976:303-304) and Graburn (1976b:10-13) make amply clear.[9] However, the craftsman producing for the tourist market often departs from motifs and style typical of the traditional art of his community. As Graburn (1976b:15) notes: "The [tourist] market itself is the most powerful source of formal and aesthetic innovation. . ." This is most obviously manifested by Makonde sculpture carved for the tourist market (Shore-Bos 1969; Stout 1966) as compared to traditional Makonde sculpture (Franz 1969), or tourist market Senufo statues (Bascom 1976:fig. 100; Himmelheber 1975:221) as compared to traditional statues (Goldwater 1964). Whether or

6

not stylistic innovations are incorporated into the esthetic vocabulary of traditional art depends, in part, upon the status of the tourist market craftsmen for, as Foster (1962:112) states, individuals with high status are more effective as innovators than those with little status. Another factor influencing whether or not artistic innovations are absorbed into traditional art depends upon the extent of the tourist market craftsman's interaction with his traditional community. If the artist has migrated in order to participate in the tourist market, his stylistic and technical innovations are lost to his community of origin. If he is perceived as a social deviant because of innovative social behavior predicated by new goals and values, his artistic innovations will not be integrated into the traditional esthetic system.[10] If he is producing items developed solely for the tourist market, such as Seri ironwood animal carvings (Ryerson 1976) or Xatitlan barkpaper paintings (Stromberg 1976), that have no function within the traditional context, they usually will not be adopted by the community regardless of the status of the innovator.

I have written above as if the role of traditional craftsman is distinct from that of tourist market producer, but this is not always so. The same individual may produce for both markets as do Laguna potters (Gill 1976:104 and 112), Lobi woodcarvers (Bascom 1976:312) and Nupe brasscasters (Nadel 1969:270).[11] The traditional craftsman who produces for both markets may devote more of his time on tourist market production because of greater demand, than on traditional commissions. Indeed, while he may have been a part-time specialist in the traditional context, the tourist market often affords the opportunity to become a full-time specialist. Full-time occupation in a craft results in better mastery of tools and material, which is reflected in changes in technique and style. The tourist market artist who also creates for the traditional market may introduce these innovations into his traditional work. Thus, participation in the tourist market can become directly responsible for changes in traditional art.

Definitions of Terms

Several terms are used throughout this book that should be defined within the context of the research. It has recently become fashionable to use Sienna in its various forms rather than Senufo (cf. Tibor 1968:28; Fagg 1971:11; Bascom 1973a:45; Rubins

1976:8), presumably following Delafosse (1908a:1:17;1912:128) who states that Senufo is a foreign term originating with the Mande-speakers to the north. Delafosse writes that Senefo/ Senofo/Senoufo are names coined by the Dyula and Bamana which mean "(those who) speak siene." Indeed, *fo* is a Mande root for the verb speak/greet. In his 1908a publication Delafosse quotes L. G. Binger (*Du Niger au golfe de Guinée par le pays de Kong et le Mossi* [1892] Paris) who claims that the dialectical variations of siene (e.g., *sene/sienou/senou*) mean "a man" in the language spoken by Senufo and "senoufo" is a contraction of Mande which means "those who say siene to signify a man." Delafosse rejects Binger's interpretation. Although the word for "person" in Sup'ide, the language spoken by northern Senufo, is *sye* (Welmers 1950:508), the word for "man" in Tyebara, Kassembele, Kufuru and Dalir, all of which are Senari dialects, is *to*. However, the word for "farmer" in Senari is *senao*, which approximates Binger's *senou*.

Delafosse (ibid.) states that not all Senufo recognize a generic term that encompasses all of them and they use the names of their "diverses tribus" rather than a generic term. However, he states it appears that a generic name exists which is Sene or, better, Siena, although it is rarely used and unfamiliar to some of the "tribus." He notes that Senufo in the Kenedougou area are called Senerhe or Sienerhe, who are located by Holas (1966:36-37) on his map of the sub-groups of Senufo. Kenedougou was an 18th century kingdom north of Korhogo, the capital of which was Sikasso from 1870 until the kingdom fell to the French in 1898 (cf. Collieaux 1924; Ferréol 1924; Person 1973b). Delafosse further claims that Sienamana is the plural of Siena and is the term used by Kenedougou Senufo to designate their nation and their various dialects. For these reasons he adopts the name Siena which he feels is the least objectionable of the various names.

Several problems are immediately apparent in Delafosse's discussions and his decision to use the term Siena. Although he rejects the name Senufo because it is of Mande origin and not used by Senufo, he accepts Siena which he states is Mande for the Senufo language. The rationale behind his rejection of one Mande word and the acceptance of another is somewhat elusive. Further, he writes that not all Senufo groups are familiar with any generic term that embraces all of them and the term Siena appears to have currency only among the Senufo in a limited area. By adopting the name Siena he imposes the name of one

Senufo group upon all Senufo, many of whom are even less familiar with Siena than they are with Senufo which they hear widely used by the Dyula living amongst them. Finally, *-mana* is neither a Senari nor Sup'ide plural suffix (cf. Welmers 1950a and b); thus Sienamana is not a plural form in either language. It is possible that in Senari, *siena-ma-na* glosses "farmers-(who) in the past-arrived (here)" or "farmers-(continue) to come-here," but this should be checked further.

Delafosse is correct in that Senufo do not have an indigenous term that encompasses all of them and the names of sub-groups are used, such as Nafambele, Kufulo, Fodombele, Kulebele and Fonombele. However, there are two terms that cut across these ethnic groupings: *senao* (plural:*senambele*) and *fijiɔ* (plural:*fijembele*). *Senambele* are groups identified with subsistence farming; *fijembele* are groups not identified with farming. Thus, Nafambele, Kufulo and Fodombele are all *senambele* and Kulebele, Fonombele and Kpeembele are *fijembele*. *Senambele* and *fijembele* state that *senambele* are the "true-true" Senufo and *fijembele* are not Senufo at all.

Regardless of what term is used to denote the population identified as Senufo in the literature, it will violate Senufo classification. Senufo has been used to indicate a population that includes both *senambele* and *fijembele* by Mande-speakers and by the West. As long as we lump groups that, to Senufo, are "unlumpable," it is better to do so with a name of foreign origins than to misuse a Senufo name. Under these circumstances, the substitution of one Mande word for another or the extension of the name of one Senufo group to embrace all Senufo is not justified.

A word of caution: at this point in our knowledge it is usually not possible to distinguish one group from the other or to know how widespread is any given feature of social organization or art inventory. Indeed, there appears to be a great deal of variation between the various Senufo groups. For example, the Nafambele, who are east and southeast of Korhogo, prefer duolocal and matrilocal residence which is rare among their neighbors who are patrilocal. The Nafambele also have a Poro masquerade complex that is very different from other Senufo groups in terms of form. Also, the Kpatobele Senufo in the Southwest are and have always been patrilineal, according to informants who are purported to be knowledgeable about them. In contrast, Senufo in the central Korhogo area are traditionally matrilineal. Thus, care must be taken that data pertaining to one group are not assumed to be valid for other groups.

The term "traditional art" is used in this text to designate objects used within the Senufo context such as paraphernalia carved for the secret societies, household items, prestige objects and objects made for traditional religious practices. Also included in this category are items such as drums carved for other African groups living in Senufoland. "Traditional art" is not meant as a stylistic determinant. European paints are often applied to pieces used by the secret societies but these pieces, too, I consider to be traditional art because they are used for traditional purposes. "Traditional artists" or "traditional craftsmen" are those producing traditional art. By "traditional art market" I mean that market which absorbs traditional art.

"Tourist art" includes all objects produced for the Western art market. Also included in this category are objects carved for educated Africans for display in their homes. The term "tourist art" includes both "commercial fine art" which Graburn (1969:3) defines as "produced to satisfy their creators and other members of the artist's society, but must also appeal to the buyers of 'primitive arts'," and "souvenir arts" in which "the artists' own tastes and traditions are subordinated to speed of production, quantity of output, and eminent saleability of the cheap product" (Graburn 1969:4). "Tourist artist" means one who produces tourist art. The "tourist art market" is that through which tourist art is channeled to non-traditional consumers.

"Antique art" and the "antique art market" are concerned with used traditional art sold for non-traditional purposes, e.g., to Western and African dealers and collectors.

Kulebeleland: Physical and Social Environments

'Senufo' is a term that has been used in the literature to designate between 600,000 and 1,000,000 individuals occupying an extended area in northern Ivory Coast, western Upper Volta and southern Mali. Their territory extends south from the Koni River north of Koutiala, Mali to Odienné, Ivory Coast in the West and from Banfora, Upper Volta to Katiola, Ivory Coast in the East. Holas (1966:15-16) indicates fifteen different geographically placed ethnic groups and four occupational "castes" (ibid:70) scattered within the geographical groupings. Welmers (1950a and 1950b) recognizes the Senufo as speaking two different languages: Senari in the South and Sup'ide in the North. He further breaks Senari down into twelve dialects (Welmers 1957), while Holas (1966:35-39) claims thirty different dialects for all Senufo.

The terrain over which they are scattered lies between eight and ten degrees north of the equator. South of Dikodougou are found the northernmost fringes of the tropical rain forest. The rest of Senufoland is gently rolling savanna occasionally interrupted by hills resulting from volcanic dikes. The entire area is studded with scrub acacia and brush interspersed by fields of yams, corn, sorghum, millet and cotton. Along water courses, wet rice is cultivated. Vestiges of primary forest are found at the edges of streams and rivers and adjacent to villages. In forests close to villages are sacred groves *(sinzang)* protected for use by secret village societies which are called Poro.[12] Two major seasons are recognized: a rainy season from May to November and a dry season from November to May. From December to April the harmattan blows off the Sahara from the East resulting in chilly (64 °F) nights and hot (100 ° + F) days.

11

The Senufo live in villages that range in size from a dozen inhabitants to large urban centers such as Korhogo. Historical events affecting the various sub-groups of Senufo have determined the type of habitation pattern. In those areas least affected by past wars and off the path of well-travelled north-south trade routes, villages are often small. In areas affected by past wars and in the path of trade caravans, villages are often large for reasons of defense and commerce and, in some cases, have populations of several thousand. Larger villages contain not only Senufo groups, but also Dyula,[13] as well as Fulani[14] who are hired by Senufo to care for Senufo cattle. Further, villages that became French administrative centers continued to expand, a phenomenon that has continued since Ivorian independence as the urban centers become foci for the collection and disbursement of goods and services.

The largest urban center in Senufoland is Korhogo which has a population of approximately 40,000. Korhogo is the administrative center for the *préfecture* of Korhogo and is a marketing and educational center as well.[15] According to Ki-Zerbo (1972:262), various Senufo clans were in Korhogo in the sixteenth century. By the eighteenth century the influence of Muslims from the north was being felt as they moved southward in pursuit of their commercial activities. The eastern campaigns of Samori, a Mande-speaking Muslim from Guinea in the late nineteenth century,[16] and his agreement with Gbon Coulibaly, chief of Korhogo, to honor a strife-free zone around Korhogo, resulted in an influx of people into the environs of Korhogo who were fleeing Samori's incursions. The French arrived at the end of the nineteenth century seeking Samori whom they captured and sent into exile in 1898. By 1908, French military operations were no longer necessary in the area (Angouvant 1908) and the Pax Francais began.

Fijembele

Ethnic groups not associated with farming are called *fijembele* (singular:*fijiɔ*). These groups are called "castes" in the literature by Gardi (1969:125), Goldwater (1964:12), Himmelheber (1963:87), Knops (1959:86), Maesen (1959:139) and Person (1970:57), who claim that *fijembele* are of lower status than farming groups. Holas (1966:127) states that Senufo "castes" do not occupy a lower social position than farmers as was once believed though he maintains that *fijembele* are restricted to marrying within their own group. Glaze (1972) questions whether the term "caste" is at all applicable and, indeed, it would not seem to be even if Berreman's (1960:120-127) flexible criteria are applied namely, hierarchical arrangement, endogamy, ascription and permanency. There is no evidence that hierarchical arrangement of *fijembele* and farmers exists and marriage restrictions are not as rigid as the literature suggests. Exogamy is not a new phenomenon but has been practiced for at least one hundred years.[17] Neither is occupation as rigidly prescribed as noted in the literature. Some *fijembele* are associated with a particular occupation but some members of any given *fijɔ* farm as well as practice the craft associated with their *fijɔ*. In some cases, *fijɔ* members farm to the exclusion of engaging in their craft.

Considerable confusion exists in the literature concerning the number, occupation and nomenclature of the various *fijembele*. Maesen (1948:139) indicates four "classes artisanales": 1) blacksmiths *("fono")*, who also do some carving; 2) casters *("lorho")*; 3) leatherworkers *("dyele")*; and 4) woodcarvers *("kule")*, who are the major suppliers of carvings. He also notes that non-artisan individuals may also carve. Knops (1959:86) claims that only one artisan group exists among Senufo, consisting of the blacksmiths who work with iron, brass, gold, clay and stone, and carve wood and ivory. However, he separates woodcarvers *("kuliu")* from blacksmiths (ibid:91), though he uses the phrase "la caste des artisans" to indicate all artisans (ibid:86). Himmelheber (1963:87) notes only three classes of artisans: 1) blacksmiths, who manufacture agricultural tools; 2) weavers; and 3) "artists," who are singers and carvers. He states that the "artists" are the lowest ranking "caste." Holas (1966:70-71) notes four "groupements professionels" engaged in industries reserved for them. They are 1) blacksmiths *("fono")*, who mine iron and fabricate iron agricultural tools, household items and weapons; 2) brassworkers *("lorho")*,[18] who use the lost wax technique *(cire perdue)* in manufacturing jewelry; 3) woodcarvers *("kpembele")*,[19] who produce ritual masks, statues and chairs; and 4) leatherworkers *("dieli")*, who are of Mande origin and not considered Senufo. They are occupied with the manufacture of saddles, boots, bags and knife sheaths. Bochet (1965:638) notes 1) *"logon,"* who cast brass, 2) *"fonobele,"* who are blacksmiths and 3) *"dallebele,"* who are woodcarvers. He does not mention other *fijembele*.

Several errors and misunderstandings appear in the above classifications. First, it is necessary to differentiate between Senufo and Dyula artisan groups and to separate Senufo nomenclature from that of the Dyula. The Dyula generally lump all artisans, with the exception of the Jelebele, under the rubric Numu. Numu are of Mande origin and may be found as far south as Agnibilikrou in the southeast corner of Ivory Coast where they are engaged in blacksmithing and carving wooden household items. However, Senufo differentiate between the artisan groups which they identify as follows:

1 Kulebele (singular: Guleo),[20] who also call themselves Dalebele (singular: Daleo). The men of this group are woodcarvers and the women specialize in mending calabashes. Dalebele is the term used on the north-south axis from Mbengue to the Dikodougou area; Kulebele is in more common usage on the north-south axis from San to Ouezoumon. Non-Kulebele in the latter area are not familiar with the term Dalebele, though Kulebele are. To the East (Mbengue to Dikodougou), non-Kulebele are familiar with either term. Dalebele state that they speak Dalir, a dialect of Senari unique to them. Kulebele in the West speak the same dialect as the farming groups among whom they live and claim they have difficulty understanding Dalir when they initially encounter it.

Dalebele and Kulebele recognize a common ancestral progenitress. They also recognize kinship with Fonombele with whom their reciprocal term of address is *fononyene*. *Fononyene* is also a generic term for Kulebele and Fonombele.

2 Fonombele (singular: Fonon), who are blacksmiths and whose major woodcarving activities are restricted to carving wooden parts of basically iron tools, e.g., hoe handles and knife handles. Fonombele are also recognized as carving "some" ritual items such as masks and statues; however, they do not carve in areas where Kulebele traditionally reside. Fonon women weave baskets and funeral mats. They recognize kinship with Kulebele, with whom they use the reciprocal term of address, *fononyene*.

3 Kpeembele (singular: Kpeo), who cast brass using the *cire perdue* method. They make brass masks, jewelry and charms. Kpeembele women are potters. Unlike Kulebele and Fonombele, they are Muslims and Dyula-speakers.

4 Jelebele (singular: Celo), who are leatherworkers. They speak a language unique to their own group, which is neither a Senari dialect nor related to other Gur languages, nor is it a Mande language. Jelebele women specialize in growing tobacco and greens. The Jelebele are rapidly becoming Muslimized with the exception of those in a few isolated villages where they are still involved in secret societies.

5 Cedumbele (also called Fa7abele, Sindumbele and Shagibele). In the Korhogo area and south of it, they are gunsmiths and blacksmiths. North of Korhogo they are weavers and blacksmiths and to the West they are engaged in weaving, gunsmithing, goldsmithing, carving and trading. Cedumbele women are potters.

These five *fijembele* are the largest artisan groups and are recognized by the general Senufo population. There are also numerous smaller *fijembele* whose existence often is not known outside of a small area.

Kulebele History and Demography

Kulebele are not found throughout Senufoland. In Ivory Coast they are concentrated in an area which forms a rough square from San in the Northwest to Ouezoumon in the Southwest and from Bougou in the Northeast to the Dikodougou area in the Southeast (See Map 1). Goldwater (1964:13) suggests that artisans among the Senufo are "survivors of an older population." This is not the case: Kulebele and Fonombele genealogies support their oral tradition that they originated in Mali and migrated southward. Oral tradition indicates the earliest southward movement was approximately 190 years ago when a Guleo left Segou to settle in Fourou, moved on to Papara, and finally settled in San.[21] Subsequent Kulebele migrations toward the end of the nineteenth century, in the eastern portion of their range, were also southward.

15

Central Northern Ivory Coast

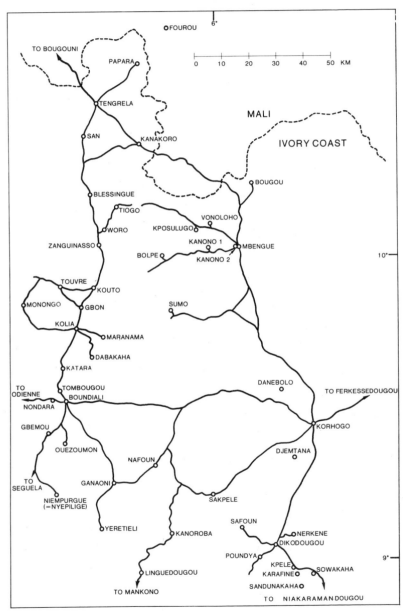

OFOUROU 6°

TO BOUGOUNI

PAPARA O

0 10 20 30 40 50 KM

TENGRELA

MALI

SAN KANAKORO

IVORY COAST

BLESSINGUE

BOUGOU

TIOGO

VONOLOHO

WORO KPOSULUGO

KANONO 1

ZANGUINASSO MBENGUE 10°

BOLPE KANONO 2

TOUVRE KOUTO

MONONGO GBON SUMO

KOLIA

MARANAMA

DABAKAHA

KATARA

DANEBOLO

TO ODIENNE TOMBOUGOU TO FERKESSEDOUGOU
BOUNDIALI

NONDARA

GBEMOU KORHOGO

OUEZOUMON DJEMTANA

NAFOUN

TO SEGUELA GANAONI

NIEMPURGUE SAKPELE
(=NYEPILIGE)

SAFOUN

YERETIELI KANOROBA NERKENE
DIKODOUGOU 9°

POUNDYA

KPELE SOWAKAHA
LINGUEDOUGOU KARAFINE

SANDUNAKAHA

TO MANKONO TO NIAKARAMANDOUGOU

16

Only the San Kulebele are still in contact with their Malian counterparts since occasional marriages are contracted between them. To the East, the oldest Kulebele village is considered to be Bolpe. Whereas Kulebele in the East claim they originated in Mali, they also state they have always been in Bolpe. Lem (1941:176) notes a major "koule" center at Ngesso which is 14 kilometers south of Sikasso, Mali, but Ivorian Kulebele have lost contact with them and are not aware of their existence. By the end of the last century, Kulebele from Bolpe began moving south and east and a few families moved west (See Map 2).

Kulebele recognize fifteen villages as being traditional Guleo settlements: San, Tiogo, Zanguinasso, Kouto, Kolia, Dabakaha, Ouezoumon, Nafoun, Djemtana, Danebolo, Korhogo, Sumo, Bolpe, Kanono and Kposulugo. A village may be occupied by ethnic groups other than Kulebele and still be designated by Kulebele as a Kulebele village. Permanent settlement in a village and two generations of Kulebele children born in it place the village in the category of traditional as opposed to one temporarily inhabited by Kulebele. With the exception of Bolpe and the two Kanono villages (designated as Kanono 1 and Kanono 2 on Map 1), all Kulebele villages are inhabited by Kulebele and at least one other ethnic group.

Originally, Bolpe contained both Kulebele and Senufo farmers. Towards the end of the nineteenth century, the Senufo chief of Mbengue raided and scattered the Senufo population in Bolpe in an attempt to throw off the yoke of Bolpe domination. The Senufo never returned. The Kulebele living in Bolpe did not flee. As an intrusive artisan group that provided household, prestige and ritual goods otherwise obtainable only with difficulty by indigenous farmers, their talents are highly valued. Thus, they were not subject to the depredations of raids and wars. As one informant described the situation: "Who is going to kill Kulebele? If the Senufo kill the Kulebele, who will carve for them? The chiefs need us to carve for them."[22] For the past eighty or more years, only Kulebele have inhabited Bolpe. At present it is reduced to four elder men and their female and pre-teenage male dependents, as the younger men have migrated.

Kanono is geographically located at two sites: the original Kanono which is indicated as Kanono 1 on Map 1, and a new Kanono founded five years ago which is adjacent to Mbengue. Old Kanono is inhabited by Kulebele and Senufo, though the Guleo population has been reduced to one elder man and his female and pre-teenage male dependents. New Kanono was founded when three elder men decided to move closer to a major highway in order that tourist art dealers might find them easily. They would be closer to public transportation to Korhogo, which, it was hoped, would deter the young men from migrating to carve for the tourist art market. They also wanted to remove themselves from the demands and threats of negative supernatural sanctions of the Kulebele chief of Old Kanono. Although Old and New Kanono are separated by twenty kilometers, the two locations are thought of by the inhabitants of both villages as socially and politically one, i.e., the political and social organization remains unchanged. Thus, the inhabitants of New Kanono maintain they are still under the hegemony of the chief who remained in Old Kanono and they conduct their affairs as though part of a single unit whereas, in fact, they enjoy considerable autonomy in their own village.

Danebolo, which is located west of Korhogo, was abandoned fifteen years ago by all the inhabitants. At one time it was populated by Kulebele, Senufo and Dyula. Kulebele claim the Dyula were responsible for its abandonment by causing illness and death. Every time a stranger moved into the village, a villager would sicken and die.[23] Most Danebolo Kulebele migrated to Korhogo.

The largest Kulebele population is found in Korhogo where more than sixty men and their dependents live. They originally occupied a large concession in Quartier Koko.[24] In the mid-1960's, the Ivorian government ordered that Korhogo be razed as a part of a redevelopment program. New streets were laid out in a grid pattern wide enough to accommodate truck and automobile traffic. Twenty-by-twenty-five-meter lots were sold, upon which the only type of construction permissible was concrete block with corrugated-metal roofs. Large enclaves of ethnic groups were allowed to purchase adjacent lots; however, the Kulebele, as was the case with other ethnic groups, were not given priority to purchase enough lots to allow all of them to remain within the defined area. Thus, some families were forced to move to new *quartiers*. Nevertheless, the largest aggregate of Kulebele still resides in its traditional location in Koko.

The size and composition of villages considered to be traditionally Kulebele are given in Table 1.

Himmelheber (1963:87) states that Kulebele (and other "castes") live in "towns" separated from the general population

18

Table 1
Populations of Traditional Kulebele Villages

Village	Population[25]	Ethnic Composition
San	1745	Kulebele, Fonombele, *senambele*, Dyula, Fulani
Tiogo	705	Kulebele, Fonombele, *senambele*, Dyula
Zanguinasso (=Zanayenekaha)	2550	Kulebele, Fonombele, Jelebele, *senambele*, Dyula, Fulani
Kouto	3825	Kulebele, Fonombele, Jelebele, *senambele*, Dyula, Fulani
Kolia	3785	Kulebele, Fonombele, *senambele*, Dyula, Fulani
Dabakaha	Approximately 1000	Kulebele, Fonombele, *senambele*, Dyula
Ouezoumon	1658	Kulebele, Fonombele, *senambele*, Dyula
Nafoun	2686	Kulebele, Fonombele, Jelebele, *senambele*, Dyula
Danebolo	Abandoned	Kulebele, *senambele*, Dyula
Djemtana	Less than 200	Kulebele, *senambele*
Korhogo	40,000	Kulebele, Fonombele, Jelebele, Kpeembele, *senambele*, Dyula, Fulani, Wolof, Hausa and various other West African strangers as well as a European population of approximately 200
Sumo	200	Kulebele, *senambele*
Bolpe	20	Kulebele
Kanono 1	104	Kulebele, *senambele*
Kanono 2	25	Kulebele (adjacent Mbengue has a mixed African population of 5032)
Kposulugo	?	Kulebele

and Knops (1959:89) also states that they reside apart, but this is not always the case. Village residence patterns are dependent upon several factors. When Kulebele migrate to a village, they are foreigners (*nubombele*; singular: *nubu*). In order to take up residence, they need to find someone, as do all strangers, to sponsor them or to act as their patron. The patron or sponsor *(jatugu)* provides housing and food for his *nubu* from whom he receives goods and services. A *jatugu* need not be a village chief *(ka7afolo)* but may be the head of an extended household. Thus, a *ka7afolo* may be a *jatugu,* but not all *jatugu* are *ka7afolo.* It is incumbent upon the *jatugu* to go through the formality of requesting permission of the *ka7afolo* to act as a *jatugu* to any given *nubu.*[26] The *jatugu* houses the *nubu* in whatever accommodations he has available. Should additional *nubombele* of the same ethnic group move into a village, they will be housed in a similar manner, creating a spatial arrangement in which the members of any given group of *nubombele* may be scattered throughout the village. If the *nubombele* become permanent residents in the village, contract marriages and expand their families, it becomes necessary to construct larger accommodations. This can be done only at the periphery of the village because of the centrifugal way by which villages expand. [27] Should additional members of the same ethnic group arrive, they take up residence with those already in residence, and the area of the village inhabited by a particular ethnic group grows until it may properly be called a *ka7a* (village). Settlements of Kulebele, whether isolated from other villages such as Bolpe, or forming a part of a larger conglomerate settlement, such as Korhogo, are called Kulebeleka7a.[28]

Thus, Kulebele are scattered among a larger population that includes other *fijembele, senambele,* Dyula and Fulani. While they are a primary source of woodcarvings for these other ethnic groups and receive land use-rights from *senambele,* both of which require interaction and reciprocal relationships with non-Kulebele, their most binding relationships are with the members of their own matrilineages.

2

Kinship
and Family Organization

The Kulebele are matrilineal and patrilocal, as are most Senufo groups. However, they have been in contact with Islam and patrilineality for many generations and some chiefly *senambele* lineages have converted to Islam and pass on political rights patrilineally. Thus, the concept of patrifiliation is not unfamiliar to Kulebele and is further reinforced by economic individualization resulting from tourist art market participation and subsequent capital investments.[29]

Kinship

The *narigba7a* (plural: *narigbaya*) is a political, religious and social unit that governs the inheritance of traditional political power and wealth, acts as a corporate group at funerals, is exogamous and controls the distribution of female members. The *narigba7a* is the matrilineage consisting of all males and females who can trace their descent from a common known progenitress. All Kulebele claim descent from a single progenitress and thus all are kinsmen, but their more immediate corporate group is that of the *narigba7a* which stands in opposition to another *narigba7a*, once the connecting female link between them has been forgotten. Segmentation of a *narigba7a* occurs when the female linking two segments is forgotten and her daughters become the earliest known progenitrices of the two segments. Holas (1966:86) states that the *narigba7a* also contains friends and slaves. This is not the case with the Kulebele. For them, the *narigba7a* is a kinship group within which membership is determined by birth.

The members of a *narigba7a* have two terms for each other which are not extended to non-*narigba7a* members: *naro* and *sheleo*. *Sheleo* is applied to all male members of the *narigba7a* who are related to Ego through a +1 or more generation female link. The reciprocal term is *naro* which is applied to males and females. All female members of the *narigba7a* are *narjao* (*naro* + *jao*:child).[30] Diagram 1 illustrates *narigba7a* kinship terminology.

Diagrams 2 and 3 illustrate kinship terms used by Kulebele from Kposulugo to the Dikodougou area (whom I shall call "eastern Kulebele" for brevity's sake) and Kulebele from San to Ouezoumon ("western Kulebele"). The differences in terminology and manner of categorization between the two reflect differing patrilineal biases. Both eastern and western Kulebele have long been exposed to Islam and its attending patrilineality. Further, the kinship system of eastern Kulebele has also been influenced by individualistic economic success in the tourist art market. While both eastern and western Kulebele appear to be in a transitional phase from matrilineality to patrilineality, they are following different patterns. Since western Kulebele have, thus far, been little affected by the tourist art market, it can be assumed that changes occurring in their kinship system are a result of Dyula-Islam-patrilineal influences. On the other hand, changes that have occurred in the eastern Kulebele system are the result of Dyula-Islam-patrilineality and new economic opportunities afforded by the tourist market.

Age takes precedence over sex in the +0 generation. *Ye7efolo* (elder sibling) is Senari and is used by eastern Kulebele. *Koro* (elder sibling) is Dyula and is used by western Kulebele. *Cono,* which indicates younger sibling, is used by both eastern and western Kulebele. While descriptive terms are used to describe kinsmen, e.g., *mi to* (my father), *mi tofoleg* (my elder father), *mi nungto* (my mother's father), terms of address cut across kinship categories. Thus, men addressed as *ba* or *aba* are +2 generation males in the *narigba7a* and the *nyeneya7asa7a* (father's *narigba7a*), +1 generation in the *nyeneya7asa7a* and +0 generation in the case of father's *naro,* who is also addressed as *aba* by western Kulebele.

Evidence for the strengthening of the patrilineage (for which there is no indigenous term) among eastern Kulebele is found in the separation of father's elder brother, by the suffix *-leg,* from father's younger brother, who is designated by the suffix *-pil* (small). Thus, rather than father and his brothers being

Diagram 1
Narigba7a Kinship Terminology

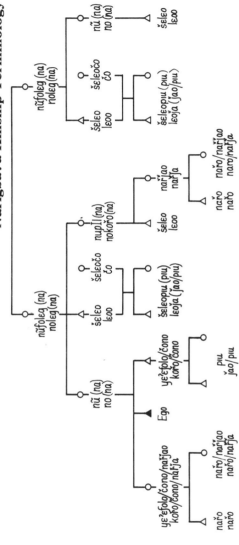

The top terms are those used by eastern Kulebele; bottom terms are those used by western Kulebele. Terms in parentheses are terms of address; where no term appears in parentheses, given names are used.

nũ̃fõlɛŋ/nolɛŋ	: old mother
nũ̃/no	: mother
nupĨĨ/nokořo	: little mother
šĕleo/lɛoo	: mother's brother
čo	: wife
yɛʔɛfõlo/kořo	: elder sibling
čono	: younger sibling
pɪu/jao	: child
nařo	: matrilineal niece or nephew
narĭjao/narĭja	: female in Ego's *narigba7a*

23

Diagram 2
"Eastern" Kulebele Kinship Terminology

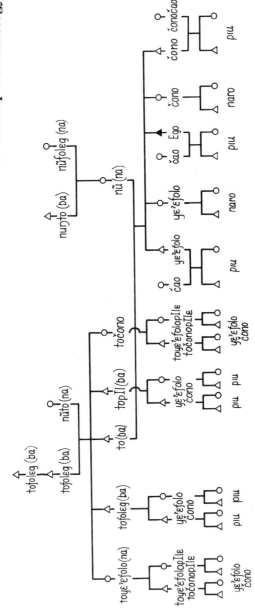

Diagram 3
"Western" Kulebele Kinship Terminology

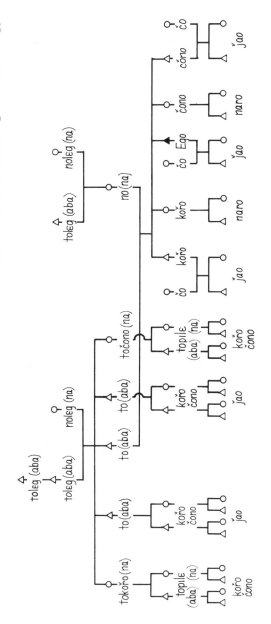

designated by one term *(to)*, as is done by western Kulebele, these individuals are hierarchically arranged with father's elder brother being lumped with the ascending males in the patriline. This phenomenon corresponds to the fact that full-brothers often share an extended household, but the eldest brother is considered to be the head of the household. Further, eastern Kulebele distinguish between +2 generation males in the patriline *(tofoleg)* and +2 generation male affines in the *narigba7a (nungto)*. In contrast, western Kulebele do not distinguish between +2 generation males in the patriline and +2 generation males affines in the *narigba7a*. Finally, eastern Kulebele separate father's mother, *nuto* (*nu:*mother; *to:*male) from mother's mother *(nufoleg)*, but western Kulebele do not distinguish between these two individuals and call both of them *noleg*. The result is that the western kinship system resembles the Hawaiian system in the +2 and +3 generations, while the eastern Kulebele rank males in the ascending generations of the patriline and isolate +2 generation females in the patriline from those in the *narigba7a*.

Marriage

Differences in marriage patterns can be detected by the use of the term of address *co* or *cao* (wife). All Kulebele use it to denote own wife as well as elder brother's wife, who is a potential wife for Ego when her husband dies. Western Kulebele also call the wife of a *sheleo* and younger brother's wife *co*, and these women are also inherited by Ego when their husband dies. Eastern Kulebele do not call either of these women *cao* and marriage with them no longer takes place, though it was practiced in the past. Although western Kulebele kinship terms do not generally reflect Islamic patrilineal influence, with the exception of the Dyula term *koro*, marriage patterns do. Ideally, *narigbaya* are exogamous: one must not marry within one's *narigba7a*. However, inconsistencies appear that can be explained only by a bias towards patrilineality. In the West there has been a general blurring of *narigba7a* boundaries in terms of maintaining strict exogamy and *narigba7a*-endogamous marriages now occur in situations where Ego and his wife are members of different *nyeneya7asaya*. Diagram 4 illustrates the differences between eastern and western Kulebele marriage patterns. Eastern Kulebele more consistently follow the principle of *narigba7a* exogamy in that no case of marriage

Diagram 4
Marriage Patterns

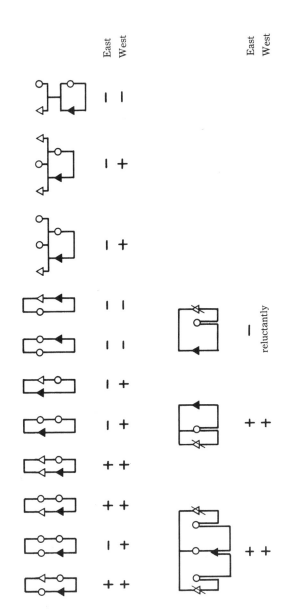

27

within the *narigba7a* is acceptable. Western Kulebele allow *naribga7a* endogamy when husband and wife have different *nyeneya7asaya*. Thus Ego may marry his mother's sister's daughter or his sister's daughter if Ego and his potential bride have different *nyeneya7asaya*. Indeed, there is evidence that among western Kulebele Ego may marry a half-sibling as long as the mother of each belongs to a different *narigba7a* or the father of each is a member of a different *nyeneya7asa7a*. One marriage was recorded where both husband and wife had the same father who was the Kulebele chief in Kolia. A second marriage had been arranged by the same chief between another son and daughter who were members of different *narigbaya*, but the girl had run away and her whereabouts were unknown.[31]

The literature stresses that Senufo artisan groups are endogamous (Bochet 1965:638; Himmelheber 1963:87; Knops 1959:92; Koffi 1966:11). But as pointed out above, they have been practicing exogamy for at least several generations. As far as Kulebele are concerned, endogamous marriages are the ideal but, in fact, exogamous marriages are not rare. However, few Kulebele women marry exogamously. Although some children are sent to live with their mother's brother *(sheleo)*, most reside in their fathers' household. Children living with their fathers usually follow his occupation and join the Poro (see Chapter 3) of their father. Thus, the labor of children with a Kulebele mother and a *senambele* father is lost to Kulebele, which results in significant problems for Kulebele cohesion and is a threat to the perpetuation of Kulebele Poro.

Kulebele response to one of their women marrying exogamously against the wishes of her *narigba7a* is the imposition of negative supernatural sanctions against the woman and the family of her non-Guleo husband. Given this response, Kulebele women are hesitant to marry exogamously, and non-Kulebele are not eager to marry Kulebele women. A *narigba7afolo* (*narigba7a* chief) sanctions an exogamous marriage for the women under his jurisdiction only if a woman is given in exchange or if a Guleo woman is given to a non-Kulebele for favors received, services rendered or to strengthen political alliances. By contrast, Kulebele men contract exogamous marriages without criticism from Kulebele: 31 per cent of 93 Kulebele marriages in which the ethnic group of the wife was recorded are male exogamous. In only three cases did family members of the non-*fiji* bride object to their daughter marrying Kulebele. In one case the girl had already been promised to someone else and in another, the girl's mother wanted her to contract the type of marriage where the girl remains with her mother and the husband has visiting and sexual privileges only. The latter type of marriage is not common to Kulebele: only two such marriages were found and in both cases they involved Kulebele women married to non-*fijiɔ* men. In the instances where the girls' families resisted their marrying Kulebele, the girls simply ran away from home and took up residence with their Kulebele husbands.

Girls are given in marriage by their *narigba7afolo* with the consent of the girl's mother and father. The circumstances under which they are given vary greatly and sometimes they are promised before they are born and have no say as to whom they will marry. An unpromised young girl is considered fortunate by her peers if she is given to a young man of her liking though the young man must meet with the approval of her *narigba7afolo* and the marriage should ideally result in strengthening desired political and economic ties.

The bridegroom performs services for and presents gifts to the mother of the girl, her father and her *sheleo*, but does not pay a brideprice. Gifts include firewood and small amounts of money (francs or cowries) for her mother; kola nuts and money are given to her *narigba7afolo* and her father. Services involve working in the fields of her *kacolofolo*, (see below) who may be her father or her *sheleo*, running errands and assisting with woodcarving, e.g., sanding, staining and carving.

The girl goes to her husband's household to live. If he has not established his own household, the young couple will reside with one of the husband's kinsmen. Precluding divorce, which is rare, the woman remains with her husband as long as she is capable of bearing children. If she is widowed while still of childbearing age, she is inherited by another male member of her husband's *narigba7a*. The inheritance of women follows from older brother to younger brother, i.e., younger brothers inherit deceased elder brothers' wives but older brothers do not ordinarily inherit deceased younger brothers' wives. Eastern Kulebele men never inherit the wives of a deceased younger brother. Western Kulebele do not like to do so but if there are no other *narigba7a* males to whom the woman can be given, they will take them, though reluctantly. It is preferable that wives of deceased younger brothers be given to the *naro*. If there are no surviving brothers to whom wives can be given, the *naro* automatically inherits them. Inheritance of a wife, however, does not require that the heir keep her. If he already has more than one wife he may keep one or two inherited women and give others to other *narigba7a* males. If a woman is widowed after menopause, she is free to return to her *narigba7a* and often establishes residence in the household of her sons.

The Kacolo

The unit of residence below village or quarter level is the *kacolo* (plural:*kacoli*) though a small village may contain only one *kacolo*. A *kacolo* is a residential group headed by a *kacolofolo* who is usually an elder male. The *kacolo* contains male and female dependents (*pibele*; singular:*piu*) of the *kacolofolo*. Most of the *pibele* of the *kacolofolo* are consanguinal and affinal kin, though the *kacolofolo* may also have *nubombele* in residence in his *kacolo*. Thus, a *kacolo* is a social grouping as well as a spatial arrangement. The members of a *kacolo* include the wives of the *kacolofolo*, their children, sons with their wives and children, and possibly the children of sisters of the *kacolofolo* (see Diagrams 5 through 7). Traditionally, one son is sent to live with his maternal uncle. Therefore, a *kacolo* could conceivably contain:

1. wives of the *kacolofolo*.
2. unmarried sons and daughters.
3. married sons, their wives and children.
4. unmarried sons of sisters of the *kacolofolo*.
5. married sisters' sons, their wives and children.

Diagram 5 illustrates a *kacolo* of this type.

Agnatic links are sometimes utilized during the process of migration. Thus, some *kacoli* contain individuals who are agnates of the *kacolofolo* such as:

6. unmarried sons of brothers.
7. married sons of brothers, their wives and children.

The composition of the Korhogo Kulebele chief's *kacolo* is illustrated in Diagram 6, which contains matrilineally related individuals as well as agnates. It will be noted that the chief *(kafu)* does not have any sisters' sons in his *kacolo*. One sister's son's *kacolo* is

Diagram 5
Kacolo Membership I

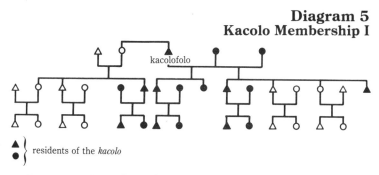

kacolofolo

▲ }
● } residents of the *kacolo*

contiguous to that of the *kafu,* but he is a *kacolofolo* in his own right as an elder male who has established his own *kacolo.* The establishment of one's own *kacolo* does not end the relationship between a new *kacolofolo* and his former *kacolofolo.* This relationship is terminated only when one of the dyad dies. Thus the sister's son *(naro)* mentioned above is still obligated to present gifts to the *kafu* who was his *kacolofolo,* which he does in the form of ceremonial clothing, money, meat and kola nuts.

There are several conjugal units of a man, his wives and their children in the *kacolo* of the Korhogo Kulebele *kafu.* Though Koffi (1966:24) and Holas (1966:86) state that Senufo call these units *gbagui,* Kulebele are not familiar with the term nor do they have a word or phrase to describe such a unit. The smallest recognized residential and domestic unit is the *kacolo.* An example of a small *kacolo* is illustrated in Diagram 7.

Impact of Inheritance and Housing Laws

A comparison of Diagram 5 with Diagrams 6 and 7 indicates how the ideal of residence with mother's brother is giving way to residence with father. This pattern is manifested in all Kulebeleka7a. The preference for patrilocal residence for sons is reinforced by two factors. First, brothers of the same mother traditionally work together and give mutual aid and support. Not all brothers of the same mother are sent to live with mother's brother. A young man living with his *sheleo* does not enjoy the same close relationship with the sons of his *sheleo* as he does with his own full-brothers, i.e., he does not become involved in close reciprocal relationships with his matrilateral cross cousins. His removal, at age seven or sometimes later, from the *kacolo* in which his brothers live does not allow him the opportunity to

31

Diagram 6
Korhogo Kulebele Chief's Kacolo Members

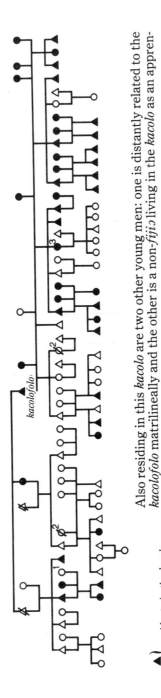

residents in the *kacolo*

Also residing in this *kacolo* are two other young men: one is distantly related to the *kacolofolo* matrilineally and the other is a non-*fijiɔ* living in the *kacolo* as an apprentice carver.

1. This woman was not moved into the *kacolo* because of the crowded conditions there.
2. This is the same individual.
3. This woman has left her husband and returned with her children to her natal *kacolo* where her mother and brother live. Ordinarily children over 5 years of age are left with their father but in this case the father is impoverished and unable to care for them.

32

Diagram 7
Kacolo Membership II

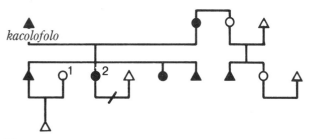

kacolofolo

$\left.\begin{array}{c}\blacktriangle\\\bullet\end{array}\right\}$ residents of the *kacolo*

Also residing in this *kacolo* is a Fonon *nubu* who is learning to carve.

1. This young woman does not get along with her husband's family. She spends her days in her father's *kacolo* and visits her husband at night.
2. This young woman left her husband.

develop close personal relationships with them. Further, he very well may not be the brother who will inherit the wives or wealth of his *sheleo,* for inheritance is generally from *sheleo* to his eldest matrilineal nephew and the eldest son is rarely sent to live with the *sheleo.* Thus, the eldest brother receives his inheritance from his *sheleo* and since he remains in his natal *kacolo,* enjoys the mutual aid and assistance of other brothers remaining in the *kacolo.* The brother sent to live with his *sheleo* inherits little and is denied the opportunity of full reciprocity with his brothers. For these reasons young men prefer remaining with their brothers, since residence with the *sheleo* confers few advantages and precludes others.

Second, Muslim custom and French civil law emphasize patrilineal descent and inheritance. The Ivorian government has adopted French laws of patrilineal inheritance. As Kulebele accumulate wealth, which is discussed more fully below, it is inherited by wives and sons. Whereas moveable wealth in the form of money and livestock can be inherited matrilineally without coming to the attention of authorities, the titles of real property, improved or unimproved, and monies in bank accounts must be passed on patrilineally. Men are now unwilling to lose the labor of sons to a wife's brother, when the son will ultimately benefit from the father's labors. Further, sons are not anxious to leave their father's *kacolo* because the absent son fears he will not share equally with his brothers. Also, brothers feel the need to present a solid front vis-à-vis half-brothers in matters of inheritance, and mothers do not want to send a son to live with a brother since it is her sons who will back her in her claims to her deceased husband's property. The result of the new inheritance laws and Kulebele accumulation of real property is that daughters are now more often sent to live with their mother's brothers than are sons since daughters do not inherit real estate.

Traditionally, each wife was provided with a thatched mud-brick dwelling *(kpa7a)* for herself and her children. Her husband had a *kpa7a* for his own use in which he entertained male friends and slept when he was not sleeping with one of his wives. A man with one wife would often not build a *kpa7a* for his personal use, but would share his wife's. In a *kacolo* consisting of more than one adult man and his wives, each wife would be provided with a *kpa7a* and the men would share a *kpa7a*. Ideally, men with more than one wife would spend four nights with one wife in her *kpa7a*, then four nights with the second wife in her *kpa7a*, etc. By the time boys are six to seven years old they are sleeping in the men's *kpa7a*. Girls remain in their mother's *kpa7a*, though in a *kacolo* that has elder women who no longer sleep with their husbands or are widowed, girls who are six or older share a *kpa7a* with an older woman.

The imposition of federal laws regulating the type of housing that can be built has resulted in some variations in living arrangements and residence patterns. Kulebele *kacoli* often are not contiguous because of the change in land distribution. The government lays out redeveloped villages in a grid pattern and sells the lots to villagers for 5,000 West African Francs (CFA) per lot, which is roughly $25.00. Villagers are sometimes given the opportunity to buy the lots upon which their *kacoli* were traditionally located but since *kacoli* were contiguous and not rectangular, government-surveyed lots rarely correspond to traditional *kacoli*. Further, the government regulates the kinds of construction materials to be used (concrete blocks and corrugated-metal roofs) and the types of houses that can be built on a lot. Prescribed are houses with a living room, two or more bedrooms and a bathing stall, which is a 4' by 5' room with a hole in the concrete floor for water drainage. Row-type apartments with one- or two-room units in them may also be constructed on the same lot with the main house. Thus, each lot is an isolable space, for it is not possible to construct buildings at random across lot boundaries as the population of the *kacolo* grows.[32]

Limitations imposed by government regulations have resulted in two major changes in residency patterns. Because the living area of the *kacolo* can no longer be added to at random, men are forced to move out and establish their own *kacolo* at a younger age than in the past. They are able to buy lots and build houses because of the income they realize from tourist art market participation. As noted above, full brothers work together and offer mutual aid. Brothers who are not able to establish independent *kacoli* often pool their resources and jointly purchase a lot and build on it.

Three types of spatially organized *kacoli* have emerged: a house in which all members of the *kacolo* live; a row-type apartment building in which units are contiguous but not inter-connecting; and a *kacolo* consisting of a house and a row-type apartment building. The first two types of *kacoli* eventually evolve into the third type. In those *kacoli* consisting solely of a house containing all the *kacolo* members, the living room, which is the spatial equivalent of the men's *kpa7a* where men entertained and slept, is the means of ingress and egress from other rooms of the house and does not offer the privacy the traditional men's *kpa7a* does. Further, bedrooms, which are the spatial equivalent of women's *kpaya,* are not large enough to allow women to receive their friends in them. Thus, the living room is used by women as well as men for receiving and entertaining. Because of the public nature of the living room, men are not willing to sleep in it. Should a *kacolofolo* have many dependents residing with him, he finds himself in the position of not having a private room, in which case he shares a bedroom with a favored wife on all nights he is not sleeping with one of his other wives. As funds become available, a row-type apartment is built behind the house, alleviating the space problem, though often the additional rooms are quickly filled with dependents and the *kacolofolo* continues to share a room with his preferred wife. Diagram 8 illustrates a *kacolo* of this type.

The above type of *kacolo* is constructed only when one elder male initiates a *kacolo*. When brothers or an elder male with married sons in residence construct a *kacolo,* the row-type apartment

Diagram 8
Spatial Arrangement of a Kacolo I

The *kacolofolo* of this *kacolo* has a small three-room house across the street. Two rooms are used for storing tourist carvings and one room is a sleeping room used by three teenage male relatives of his first wife's and a *nubu*. Even though these young men are spatially separated from the rest of the *kacolo* they are still members of it.

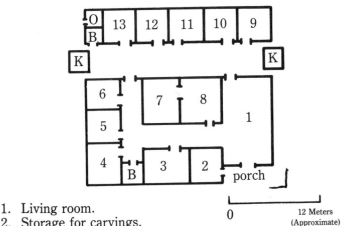

1. Living room.
2. Storage for carvings.
3. *Kacolo* and first wife.
4. Second wife and infant.
5. Sister's son and deceased wife's son of the *kacolofolo*.
6. Guest room for visiting kinsmen.
7. Third wife.
8. First wife's prepubertal daughters and teenage daughter of her sister's.
9. Second wife's cooking utensils, food and storage.
10. First wife's cooking utensils, food and storage.
11. Storage for carvings. Previously rented as a sleeping room to a Dyula tailor.
12. Storage for carvings.
13. Third wife's cooking utensils, food and storage.
B. Bathing rooms.
O. Outhouse.
K. Kitchens.

is built on the back of the lot first. This allows each man and his wives separate units. However, as dependents increase, crowding occurs, and again it is necessary that men share sleeping quarters with a wife as in Diagram 9. Ultimately, a house which will become the men's house will be built on the front portion of the lot and the units on the rear of the lot will be used by the women.

Men's and Women's Roles

Work is assigned on the basis of age and sex. Elder males supervise and coordinate all the activities in their *kacolo;* they delegate chores and regulate economic pursuits. The only subsistence activity they admit to being directly involved in is the buying and selling of livestock: cattle, goats, sheep, chickens and guinea fowl. In rural areas they distribute land for farming, the use-rights of which they obtain from the farmers who first settled the land. They also delegate carving commissions for traditional items, except for commissions received directly by a carver from a consumer. While Korhogo Kulebele engage in less farming than their rural brethren, due to lack of land and because they prefer to carve for the tourist art market, the role of the *kacolofolo* as work coordinator has not changed. Neither has his obligation of providing meat, clothing and medical treatment for members of his *kacolo* changed except that now adult male members of his *kacolo,* who command more wealth than in the past, provide clothing and sometimes medical care, which may be traditional or western, for their wives and children.

By the time a youth reaches his late teens, he has mastered the techniques of and is engaged in all the subsistence activities in which men participate until they become elders. These include clearing fields for farming and preparing them for planting by building ingyam hills[33] or elevated rows for corn, millet, sorghum or peanuts; chopping down trees for firewood and splitting the larger branches and trunks; and carving. Younger teenage boys help the women in the fields, herd livestock, sand and stain carved items, and are actively engaged in learning to carve. They also repair hut walls and thatch huts with thatching that has been tied together by a hired specialist. These latter activities are supervised by older teenage boys and young men. Further, they assist specialists who are hired to build mud-brick huts *en brousse* and

Diagram 9
Spatial Arrangement of a Kacolo II

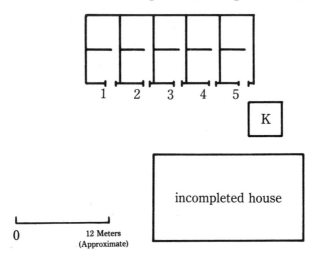

1. Younger brother of the *kacolofolo* and his wife and two children.
2. First and third wives of *kacolofolo* and one infant.
3. *Kacolofolo* and third wife.
4. Father's son and his wife and infant.
5. Wimosiso, 2 fasoso, wifabrso and two young sons of the *kacolofolo*.
K. Kitchen.

The male kinsmen in 5 have migrated to Korhogo to attend secondary school.

The younger brother in 1 took a second wife after I left Korhogo. It is not known where she is sleeping.

concrete-block houses in Korhogo, which saves on the cost of labor. Younger boys run errands, collect firewood and help in the fields and with the livestock.

Women's work is more varied than men's. Elder women engage in the petty marketing of sauce ingredients in local markets, spin cotton thread which they sell in the market and mend calabash containers. The latter is a skill practiced only by Kulebele women. Non-Kulebele are dependent upon them to keep their calabash bowls, spoons, water pots and snuff jars in repair. Imported plastic items such as buckets and tubs are also repaired by Kulebele women using the same awls, fibers and techniques they employ for repairing calabashes. By the time a woman is in her early twenties, she can spin and repair calabashes and plastic containers, but these activities are more generally done by older women who no longer work in the fields.

Younger women work in the fields. They do the planting, weeding, harvesting and headloading of the crop back to the *kacolo*. It is the women who are responsible for providing grains, ingyams and sauce ingredients for the family diet, though this has changed in the urban context where land use-rights are difficult to obtain. In both the rural and urban context, women chop firewood, haul water and cook for themselves and their children. Cooking for the men of the *kacolo* is taken in turn by the women and is dependent upon how many women are in residence in proportion to the number of men.

Women also sell kindling, which they lay out in small stacks in front of their houses, and sometimes sell cooked food such as fried cakes, ingyams and roasted groundpeas and peanuts. If husbands or other kinsmen wish to partake of the prepared food, they must pay for it, for the preparation of cooked food to sell is an economic endeavor of women and is independent of the dietary needs of the *kacolo*. The monies realized from marketing activities, container repairing, spinning and the sale of kindling and cooked food are always small in scale, but they provide women with cash with which they buy sauce ingredients, if they do not have a garden space as is common in the urban situation, jewelry, cosmetics and shoes for themselves and their children. As noted above, men are responsible for buying clothing, but this does not include shoes.

Teenage girls work in the fields, haul water and assist with cooking. They collect firewood but are not allowed to use the heavy axes used by more adult women for fear they will injure themselves. They are under the general supervision of older female *kacolo* members. Prepubertal girls collect scraps of firewood and run errands for their mother. Their time is spent mostly at play which frequently mimics the activities of their mother.

Babies are cared for almost exclusively by their mother. Elder kinswomen and young girls carry babies on their backs from time to time but the feeding and bathing of infants is done by the mother.

Women in rural areas are still responsible for providing the *kacolo* with basic staples such as ingyams, rice, corn, peanuts and millet. However, in Korhogo, to which Kulebele carvers have been attracted because of economic opportunities, there is little land available for strangers as a result of population pressures and cash-cropping. Thus, Kulebele women in Korhogo rarely undertake farming ventures. They mend calabash containers, spin and engage in petty marketing which activities provide them with pocket-money for sauce ingredients, shoes and funeral gifts, but the bulk of the family diet is purchased with money earned by men's carving. Cooking, which is done on a rotational basis, sweeping, washing their own clothes and those of their young children, chopping firewood and infant care are the only other activities which engage their attention. A great deal of their time is spent gossiping, visiting and plaiting one another's hair. Men complain frequently and bitterly that their women are idle. "All they do is sleep and not work. How are they going to find money if they don't work?" complained a Guleo. One of the two instances of wife-beating I was aware of in two-and-one-half years with Kulebele occurred when a husband accused his wife of being lazy and spending all of her time gossiping and not cooking and looking after their five children.

In an effort to get women to work, young girls are encouraged to find housework for wealthy Dyula or strangers, which places them outside the jurisdiction of the *kacolofolobele* for approximately ten to twelve hours each day. Since this practice has been occurring only since the early 1970's, it is too soon to tell what kinds of effects it will have, though complaints are made that these girls are "trop bandit," difficult to handle and do not have any respect for anyone. Men also send their wives and younger female dependents to work for wages in farmers' fields around Korhogo or to rural villages to help kinsmen in the fields. Thus, women have been introduced to the concept of wage work and are allowed to keep part of their earnings but they prefer to stay home. They have little to spend their money on since their husbands and fathers provide them with food, clothing and housing paid for by tourist market earnings. "Why should we work? Our men find lots of money," stated a young wife. Men are dismayed and angry at their wives' idleness, accuse them of being lazy and state that if it were not for the fact that they want children, they would not marry but would satisfy their sexual needs by visiting "les filles en ville." Visiting a prostitute, they claim, is cheaper than maintaining a wife and prostitutes do not endlessly nag for money. Thus, because of increased wealth realized through participation in the tourist market and the lack of land around Korhogo, the economic spheres once the responsibility of women and those formerly the responsibility of men, have broken down. Men are assuming financial responsibilities once held by women and women no longer contribute economically to the maintenance of the household.

Although the patrilineage does not exist as a corporate group and there is no indigenous term for a patrilineal grouping, the kinship terms of eastern Kulebele and marriage patterns of western Kulebele indicate a strengthening of agnatic relationships and violation of the traditional insistence of *narigba7a*-exogamous marriage. While the levirate is still being practiced, though with some modifications among eastern Kulebele, there is now competition between sons and *narobele,* and among half-brothers, for other forms of wealth. However, in spite of patrilineal inheritance of goods, the *narigba7a* still retains political prerogatives as we shall see in the chapter that follows.

3

Political
Organization and Poro

While the *kacolo* is the primary economic unit, the *narigba7a* is the primary political and ritual unit. Ideally, each *narigba7a* has a Poro, the leader of which is also head of the *narigba7a*. Thus decisions concerning sacred and secular affairs of the *narigba7a* are in the hands of one man, the *narigbafolo* (*narigba7a* + *folo:* owner), whose authority and decisions are confirmed and implemented by the *narigba7a* Poro.

Political Organization

Chieftainship is passed down through the *narigba7a* from the oldest brother to younger brothers and then to sisters' sons *(narobele)* in strict accordance with the age of the men. Order of inheritance of chieftainship by *narobele* is in accordance with their birth order and not dependent on the relative ages of the mothers. The *narigbafolo* is the eldest living male of a *narigba7a*. His authority extends over members of his *narigba7a* who, by reason of patrilocality, are scattered throughout many *kacoli* and villages. The *narigbafolo* is responsible for mediating intra-*narigba7a* disputes; he determines the disposal of the females of his *narigba7a;* he represents his *narigba7a* vis-à-vis other *narigbaya;* he is the organizer of funerals for *narigba7a* members; he is the ritual leader of his *narigba7a* and the chief source of protection from malevolent supernatural forces. He also can impose supernatural sanctions against Kulebele and non-Kulebele.

Where male members of more than one *narigba7a* reside in a village, chieftainship is vested in the first *narigba7a* to settle in the village. A *kafu* (*ka7a*:village + *folo*) is the head of all Kulebele *kacoli* in the village, which includes members of various *narigbaya*. Thus, a *kafu* is the ultimate authority over a geographically definable space occupied by a heterogeneous grouping of people, while the authority of a *narigbafolo* extends over a homogeneous group of people, members of the *narigba7a*, who are disbursed throughout Kulebeleland. When inter-*kacolo* or -*narigba7a* conflicts occur, they are mediated by the *kafu*, who is entitled to gifts of money, food and livestock from those under his jurisdiction. The *kafu* can also command the labor of all of his *pibele* (children, dependents) and particularly that of the members of his Poro. He is not only a political personage, but also organizes the ritual activities of his *pibele* and has knowledge of supernatural techniques by which he protects those Kulebele under his hegemony. He also has malevolent supernatural forces at his disposal, which can be directed at Kulebele and non-Kulebele.

Acting in concert with the *kafu*, but of lesser authority, are elder males who belong to the same Poro age grade as the *kafu*. These men are usually *kacolofobele*, though not all *kacolofobele* rank with the elders. Ranking is dependent upon one's membership in the succession of Poro age grades; it is passed along according to *narigba7a* membership as noted above.

Migration in search of work has long been customary with Kulebele. When men migrate, their political and ritual rights and obligations remain operative within the political and ritual sphere of their *narigba7a* and their *kafu*, which may or may not be mutually exclusive categories. Thus, men who have migrated to Korhogo from Kolia, for example, are primarily involved with their rights and obligations as *pibele* of the Kolia Kulebele *kafu*, who is also their *narigbafolo*, and their involvement with the Korhogo *kafu* is secondary even though some of them are members of the latter's Poro. A *kafu* enumerating his *pibele* notes those no longer residing in his village. In some instances, two *kafobele* will claim jurisdiction over the same man. One claim could be made on the basis of lineage membership, patrilocality or avunculocality as opposed to a second claim based upon immigrant residence and Poro participation. Thus, a Guleo may be beholden to more than one Kulebele chief; his obligations are determined by kinship and residence.

Knops (1959:91) states that Senufo artisan groups govern neither their own quarters nor villages but are submissive to ruling farmer groups. This is not the case. Not only do they have their own political structure, which is autonomous from farmer groups and other *fijembele,* but it is also possible for *fijembele* to become *kafobele* over farmers through Kulebele male exogamous marriage to a female of a ruling farmer *narigba7a.* Diagram 10 illustrates a case in which a Guleo would have become *kafu* of a farmers' village except for the fact of emigration. When *kafu* A died, B became *kafu.* When B died, C was in line to become *kafu,* but he had emigrated to Abidjan and was not willing to return to the village to assume chieftainship. E, whose mother was a member of the ruling farmer *narigba7a* and whose father was a Guleo, was next in line of succession. As a boy, E had lived with B, for whom he had cared for livestock and from whom he had learned to farm. However, he had also lived with his father, who had taught him how to carve. E preferred the occupation of carving and earned a reputation as a fine carver of Poro masks and other ritual paraphernalia. Ultimately he emigrated to Korhogo, where he and his younger brother, F, were deeply committed to carving for the tourist art market. E and F identified themselves as Kulebele and were initiates in Kulebele Poro. Neither had been initiated in a farmer Poro. The village elders determined that E was next in line for the chieftainship and asked him to become *kafu.* However, he was not willing to move to the village. His tourist art market participation was far more lucrative than farming *en brousse* and his responsibilities as a *kafu* would have taken much time away from his carving. Neither was F willing to leave Korhogo to become *kafu* in a rural village. Their sister's son was a school boy and not old enough to be a *kafu.* E suggested that D act as *kafu,* which was acceptable to the villagers, with the understanding that should E ultimately decide to move to the village, he could reclaim his position as *kafu.* Although E is a member of the ruling farmer *narigba7a* in this case, he is occupationally and ritually identified as a Guleo.

Another instance of a *fijio* becoming *kafu* over farmers involves the celebrated Gbon Coulibaly who was *kafu* of Korhogo and a large surrounding area that included 112 villages when the French arrived at the end of the nineteenth century (Fiches Signalétiques des Chefs Indigènes 1918). Coulibaly inherited his chieftainship from his father as a result of northern Muslim interference. His mother was a member of the first Fonombele *narigba7a* to settle in Korhogo, which provided the Fonombele *kafubele.* Thus, Coulibaly was *kafu* over a sizeable *senambele*

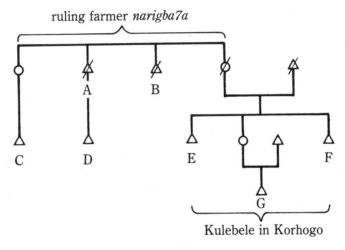

Diagram 10
Inheritance of Chieftainship by Kulebele

ruling farmer *narigba7a*

A B

C D E F

G

Kulebele in Korhogo

population and his matrilateral parallel cousin was *kafu* of the Korhogo Fonombele: both men were members of the same *fijiɔ narigba7a*. Chieftainship of the Korhogo *senambele* has continued to be inherited patrilineally but, in this case, the *senambele kafubele* continue to marry Fonombele women. Thus, subsequent *senambele kafubele* are members of Fonombele *narigba7a* and participate in Fonombele rituals.

Poro Age Grades

Poro are secret societies to which all post-pubertal males and post-menopausal females belong.[34] Every Senufo sub-group has its own Poro marked by specific traditions, history, symbolism, dances, musical instruments and music, ceremonies, initiation system and maskers.[35] While the general configuration of Poro is similar within any one sub-group, each has several Poro sections or "lodges." Thus, there is a Kulebele Poro which is unique in its body of beliefs, paraphernalia and protocol, and thirteen Kulebele Poro lodges, each headed by the chief of a maximal lineage and each embellishing the major Kulebele Poro themes in a slightly different way. An individual is not knowledgeable about all the complexities of any Poro except those of which he is a member. It is possible to join as many Poro as one wishes, but since the training and initiation periods span from six-and-one-half to twenty-one years, few individuals belong to more than two and many join only one.

Poro is a vehicle for instilling social values and disciplining recalcitrant young men. It is a means of tuning young men to a peak of physical fitness and stamina in order that they will be able to withstand the hardships of three days and nights of rigorous funeral rituals and dancing, during which they have little time to eat or sleep. The institution of Poro reinforces political organization and validates the rights of elders. It is a source of income for elders. Becoming a Poro elder is a form of social security in that initiation fees of money, livestock, ingyams and grains, and money collected at funerals are divided among the elders. Further, it is the means by which the dead are separated from the living through obligatory and complex funeral ceremonies.

The Kulebele Poro are divided into three age grades and the elders who have passed through all three. A new age set is initiated every six-and-one-half years, at which time the previous three age sets are promoted to the next grade. The lowest grade consists of young teenage boys whose Poro responsibilities are light and are mainly concerned with learning the dances, how to braid the leather quirts they will use when they are promoted to the next age grade, the maintenance of equipment, and how to play the rasps *(kori)*, flute *(man)* and the two different-sized drums used by Kulebele.[36] They are also called upon to run errands for men in the higher grades and to help funeral masqueraders dress. Their secular duties include farm labor, caring for livestock and performing simple carving tasks. Inclusion in this age grade requires gifts of small livestock, ingyams, rice and other grains, and money; the amount of money, number of livestock and amount of other gifts is fixed. Since boys do not have personal resources to provide these gifts, their *narigba7a* provides them. By the time they are ready to begin the second age grade, they are income-producing and are expected to provide their own initiation fees.

The second age grade consists of young men between approximately 18 and 25 years of age. This grade is responsible for the bulk of physical activities such as transporting musical instruments and dance paraphernalia to funeral sites. Funerals are held in the *kacolo* of the *narigbafolo* of the deceased, which often requires transporting Poro equipment 120 kilometers or more. Traditionally, funeral gear was headloaded by Poro initiates on foot, a practice still current among many Senufo. However, Kulebele now transport Poro gear on motorbikes which most Kulebele have by the time they are in their early twenties. Kulebele are able to buy motorbikes at such a relatively young age because of the earnings they realize from tourist art market participation; most young farmers are not able to earn enough money to buy motorbikes and, in fact, most elder male farmers cannot afford to buy a motorbike.[37]

Members of the second age grade are also responsible for dancing Poro masks at funerals and for providing the music. They also maintain the drums, masks and costumes. During the funeral festivities and rites they must run errands for their elders, maintain the round of funeral activities, see that honored guests are comfortable and fed, and during the dancing of the masks, solicit and collect the money from onlookers which will be redistributed among the elders. The success of a funeral lies in the following of prescribed rites for a period of three days and nights by members of this age grade, during which time its members must get by with only snatches of sleep. Their reward for their efforts is provided by the *narigba7a* of the deceased in the form of pots of *sim,* a beer made of millet and/or sorghum liberally laced with hot pepper. Their secular duties include heavy farm labor, where Kulebele are farming, and assisting their elders with carving.

The third age grade consists of men who have completed the second age grade. Their duties include overseeing the activities of the second age grade and training the first age grade in matters of funeral protocol and discipline. Their involvement in funerals is far less intense than that of the second grade. Kulebele in the first and second grades liken the men in the third grade to military officers who observe and give instructions. They very often participate in music-making at funerals, an activity they enjoy, but this is also necessary because none of the Kulebele Poro has enough men in the second grade to perform all the necessary duties and to be responsible for music-making too. Since music-making requires the least amount of physical effort as compared to dancing masks and transporting equipment, music-making is considered to be a more appropriate activity for the third age grade. However, a few men in the third grade also dance masks from time to time, not because they are required to, but because they enjoy it or are particularly fine dancers. The third and last day of every funeral is devoted to a mask-dancing competition between participating Poro, each of which puts forth its very finest dancer who is often a third age grade man. Men in the third grade receive a small portion of the money collected during the funeral rites.

The last stage of being a Poro member is that of elder. An elder is an observer and the recipient of a share of money collected at funerals and fees collected from new initiates. He may interfere during the funeral rites if he feels they are not being conducted properly, but his role is basically passive within the funeral context.[38]

Poro as an Instrument of Political and Economic Manipulation

Each of the Kulebele villages listed in Table 1 has its own Poro, though not all are currently active in terms of initiation and public funeral rites. Ouezoumon, where only three adult male Kulebele are left, and San and Zanguinasso, are unable to maintain their Poro because of lack of recruitable initiates. While they are able to meet most of their ordinary ritual needs, they do not have the manpower to conduct the all-important funeral rites necessary to separate the dead from the living and to send the *pigele* (souls; singular:*pil*) of their dead on their way to the village-of-the-dead *(kulyeebele ka7a)*. At present there are twelve Kulebele Poro still initiating members: Tiogo; Kouto; Kolia; Dabakaha; Nafoun; Djemtana;[39] Korhogo; Sumo; Danebolo; Bolpe; Kposulugo and Kanono.

Kulebele without active Poro must depend upon kinship ties and political alliances with Kulebele who have Poro to perform at their funerals. They also join *senambele* Poro which obligates these Poro to perform at their funerals. Ideally, however, funerals are hosted by the *narigba7a* Poro of the deceased and Kulebele *narigbaya* that have too few members to maintain a Poro also do not have the economic or manpower resources to host elaborate funerals which requires feeding all the funeral guests and enough males to perform all of the duties noted in the preceding section. An absolute minimum of eight initiates in the second age grade is necessary to conduct a Kulebele funeral, but a membership this low requires an ample membership in the first and third age grades for assistance, which results in boys performing tasks they are not thoroughly knowledgeable about and men participating in activities that are ordinarily below their Poro ranking. For these reasons it is incumbent upon *narigbafobele* to maintain their Poro by recruiting as many new initiates as possible. Further, the second age grade is an important source of labor in the fields and carving and all three age grades are sources of initiation fees which are divided among the elders.

Poro membership is drawn from several potential sources. Ideally, boys join the Poro of their *narigba7a* and the core membership of any Poro is that of male members of the *narigba7a* associated with it. However, the custom of migrating in search of work results in boys residing at considerable distances from their *narigba7a* Poro. Thus, some boys are initiated into their father's Poro or the Poro of their *kafu*. Also, non-Kulebele may join Kulebele Poro, although the only such instances of which I am aware have occurred recently and involved *senambele* boys and young men who have been accepted as carving apprentices by Kulebele. If second and third age grade males are already members of a Poro and migrate, they are required to participate in the Poro of their new *kafu* for a year. If they wish to promote an alliance with their new *kafu* they continue to participate in his Poro. For example, one young man from Djemtana was a Djemtana Poro initiate in the second age grade and migrated to Korhogo where he was obligated to participate in the Korhogo Kulebele Poro for a year, much to his disgust; he was jealous of the wealth and cohesiveness of the Korhogo Kulebele. On the other hand, a third age grade man, an initiate of the Bolpe Kulebele Poro, was more active in the Korhogo Kulebele Poro: he had migrated to Korhogo when he was 12 and had initially joined the Korhogo Kulebele Poro which was headed by his father's brother, an important and wealthy Kulebele *kafu*. Thus, while joining a Poro is obligatory, the choice of which lodge is somewhat flexible and depends upon kinship ties and residence. This flexibility makes it possible for *kafubele* to compete with each other for Poro members, whose labor and initiation fees enrich the elders and give status to the *kafu*.

Oral tradition in Senufoland records a history of conflict between Poro in which confrontations have occurred, some of which have resulted in the migration of entire groups. Glaze (1976:35-36) records a Jelebele tale in which they were forced out of Kong, an old and important Dyula trade and religious center in Northeast Ivory Coast until Samori demolished it in 1897, because of conflict between their Poro and the Dyula. Another Jelebele tradition tells of a conflict between another of their Poro and a *senambele* Poro in which the latter were angered because the Jelebele Poro had learned the technique of fire-walking which they would not share with the *senambele* Poro. *Senambele* Poro songs in Korhogo tell of conflict between the Poro of its *senambele* founder and a Fonon who was refused funeral rites for one of his kinsmen because the Fonon was not an initiate of the *senambele* Poro. Angered, the Fonon started his own Poro.

The potential for conflict is manifested between Kulebele Poro by the competitive mask-dancing on the final day of Kulebele funerals in which the elders judge the dancing, declare a winner and rank the other maskers according to how well they danced. The dancers that are judged wear the same type of mask and costume, dance to the same music and perform the same dance. While the Poro of the *narigba7a* hosting the funeral inevitably wins the contest, a margin of doubt exists, which resulted in an eruption of hostilities at a Kulebele funeral in Nafoun in 1975 attended by several Kulebele Poro lodges including the one from Korhogo. On the first day of mask-dancing, the Korhogo Kulebele Poro performed particularly well—so well, that the Nafoun Kulebele Poro feared that Korhogo would win the dance competition on the final day. The Nafoun Poro asked the Korhogo Poro for the secret of their fine dancing, the source of which they assumed was supernatural. The Korhogo Poro refused to divulge their secret and the Nafoun Poro, seeking an advantage in the dance competition, employed and paid a *senambele* "sorcerer"[40] to impede the Korhogo Poro maskers during the dance contest. As a result, a Korhogo masker was stricken while dancing and fell to the ground, unable to speak and unable to control his twitching body. One of the masker's attendants was also afflicted at the same time. Both claimed they would have not been affected by the Nafoun machinations if they had been under the protection of their *narigbafolo* in Kolia, rather than their Korhogo Kulebele *kafu* and his Poro.

A third age grade initiate of the Korhogo Kulebele Poro, who was a son of the Korhogo Kulebele *kafu*, administered some "medicine" imbued with supernatural healing powers to the fallen dancers, who recovered quickly, but the entire Korhogo entourage, which included women and children, left Nafoun immediately and returned to Korhogo where the incident was reported to the Korhogo Kulebele *kafu*. The *kafu* divined the cause of the seizures and declared that his Poro would never again participate in Kulebele funerals in Nafoun. However, he also stated that individuals under his suzerainty could visit Nafoun to visit kinsmen, attend funerals or buy Nafoun carvings for sale in the tourist art market.

Nafoun is an important source of carvings for Kulebele who are tourist art market dealers, many of whom have passed through all three age grades of the Korhogo Kulebele Poro, are *pibele* of the Korhogo Kulebele *kafu* and belong to the same *narigba7a* as the *kafu*. This *kafu* is also a tourist art market dealer and buys carvings from Nafoun Kulebele. Had he severed all ties with Nafoun Kulebele, an important source of carvings would have been eliminated. By allowing his *pibele* to attend Kulebele funerals in Nafoun he also allowed the flow of funeral gifts, such as cloth, food and money, to continue from his *narigba7a* to Nafoun. Thus, the sanctions he employed were ritualistic, not economic. However, Djemtana Kulebele, who are allies of the Korhogo Kulebele and who do not buy carvings from Nafoun, closed all avenues of interaction between themselves and Nafoun Kulebele in retaliation for the Nafoun attack on Korhogo. A man from Nafoun, who visited a kinsman in Djemtana in spite of Djemtana Kulebele warnings, was struck blind, for which Djemtana Kulebele take credit.

There is evidence that the Nafoun Kulebele Poro was not simply reacting to superior dancing by the Korhogo Kulebele Poro. The Korhogo Kulebele *kafu* is known to be extremely wealthy in terms of *pibele,* cattle, tourist art market inventory and improved real estate. Indeed, he is the wealthiest of all Kulebele *kafubele* and is the object of many jealousies by those who are neither members of his *narigba7a* nor dependents of his. Further, he and several of the Kulebele under his suzerainty, which includes two favored sons who are partners with their father as tourist art market dealers, are deeply disliked because they pay poorly for the carvings they buy and usually do not pay in full. This same *kafu* is accused of expansionistic behavior in terms of recruiting initiates for his Poro and widening his politico-economic influence over Kulebele who do not consider themselves beholden to him. His success in his endeavors is purportedly realized because he implements supernatural means to achieve his goals. While sharp business practices, such as not paying in full, and the implementation of supernatural powers to achieve success are both acceptable when directed at out-groups, they should not be used against members of one's own group. Thus, ideally, Kulebele should not exploit other Kulebele.

The contention that decisions of the Korhogo Kulebele *kafu* concerning relations with Nafoun were influenced by the economic needs of himself and his *pibele* as tourist art market dealers is supported by a case of conflict between Korhogo Kulebele and Danebolo Kulebele. Again, the Korhogo Kulebele *kafu* is one of the major participants.

Kulebele from Danebolo emigrated *en masse* at the end of the 1950's or early in the 1960's because of numerous illnesses and deaths believed to have been instigated by Dyula. The Danebolo Kulebele migrated to Korhogo in order to be close to tourist art market dealers. The Korhogo Kulebele *kafu* provided the immigrants with space to build their houses in and around his *kacolo* and gave them space in his *sinzang* (sacred woods) where they built their Poro huts. Because the entire Danebolo Kulebele population and *kafu* were in Korhogo, their Poro masks, costumes, musical instruments and other paraphernalia were transported to Korhogo where they intended to establish their Poro. The Korhogo Kulebele *kafu* also gave one of his daughters to a Danebolo male who was third in line for the chieftainship of the Danebolo Kulebele and when the Ivorian government sought carvers to work at the national museum in Abidjan the Korhogo Kulebele *kafu* offered one of the positions to the Danebolo Kulebele.

As *narigbafolo* of the first Kulebele *narigba7a* to settle in Korhogo, the Korhogo Kulebele *kafu* was the primary Kulebele *kafu* in Korhogo and ordinarily the Danebolo migrants would have fallen under his suzerainty. However, their *kafu,* an elderly man widely respected because of his wisdom and supernatural powers, had migrated with them. The Korhogo Kulebele *kafu* attempted to implement a political alliance with the Danebolo *kafu,* rather than to absorb him and his *pibele* into his own sociopolitical system. Indeed, the two *kafubele* cooperated by sharing immigrant rural Kulebele initiated into their Poro. Thus, two brothers from Kolia, who immigrated to Korhogo and had no kinship or other social ties with either *kafu,* each joined a different Kulebele Poro in Korhogo; one is a Danebolo Kulebele Poro initiate and the other is an initiate in the Korhogo Kulebele Poro.

Subsequently the Danebolo Kulebele *kafu* died. The next man in line to be *kafu* was very elderly and had elected to live in a village adjacent to Danebolo. He delegated his duties as *kafu* to his eldest *naro* (sister's son) who lived in Korhogo and was an elder in the Danebolo Kulebele Poro. The *naro,* however, was considerably younger than the Korhogo Kulebele *kafu,* who apparently decided that the time was propitious for attempting to incorporate Danebolo Kulebele under his suzerainty by requiring that all of the men who had not completed all three Danebolo Poro age grades become initiates in his Poro. The scheme was rejected by the Danebolo Kulebele and a confrontation occurred between the Korhogo Kulebele *kafu* and the Danebolo *naro* in which the former claimed he had been insulted. As a result, he declared that his Poro would not perform at Danebolo funerals until an apology was forthcoming. The *naro* has never apologized and the Korhogo Kulebele Poro does not perform at Danebolo funerals, nor does the Korhogo Kulebele *kafu* allow any of his *pibele* to attend Danebolo funerals as spectators. He threatens to use supernatural sanctions against them if they do. Thus, the Korhogo *kafu* has effectively denied the Danebolo Kulebele the ritual support of his Poro at their funerals and has prevented the flow of funeral gifts of money, cloth and livestock from his larger, wealthier *narigba7a* to the smaller, poorer Danebolo *narigba7a.* Indeed, his daughter left her Danebolo husband and moved back to her father's *kacolo* after, according to Kolia informants, she had milked her husband of all his money which she gave to her father and mother.

In 1975 the Danebolo Kulebele *kafu* died and the chieftainship passed on to the daughter's husband: the *naro* of the deceased chief no longer is acting-*kafu.* As of October 1975 there had been no reconciliation between the two *kafubele,* although the Danebolo *kafu* was attempting to open an avenue of communication with the Korhogo Kulebele *kafu* by visiting his house every morning and evening to extend formal greetings, which were not reciprocated. Indeed, within the context of rank and formal greeting behavior the Danebolo Kulebele *kafu* signaled the higher status of the Korhogo Kulebele *kafu* by calling on him. Although the Korhogo *kafu* did not return the greetings, his daughter occasionally took prepared food to her husband, the Danebolo Kulebele *kafu,* the ingredients for which had been provided by her father.

The conflict between Danebolo and Korhogo Kulebele is a graphic example of politico-economic conflict resulting from tourist art market exploitation. The Danebolo Kulebele decision to migrate to Korhogo was stimulated by a desire to participate in the new lucrative art market that made it possible for large numbers of carvers to congregate. In the past it was necessary that Kulebele space themselves throughout Senufoland in order to avoid competing with one another and there is no instance where more than one Kulebele *kafu* resided in a village. The *narigbafolo* of the first Kulebele *narigba7a* to settle in a village was always pre-eminent among the Kulebele in that village and migration was generally to villages where there were no Kulebele in residence. Thus, Kulebele *kafubele* were widely spaced which limited the possibility of politico-economic conflict.

The presence of the Danebolo Kulebele in Korhogo, with their independent Poro and political organization, neither enhanced the status nor expanded the political base of the Korhogo Kulebele *kafu*. Only by initiating the Danebolo Kulebele into his own Poro could the Korhogo Kulebele *kafu* extend his suzerainty over the migrants and enrich his own *narigba7a* from the labors of the new initiates and their initiation fees. His alliances with other Kulebele groups guaranteed the participation of their Poro at Korhogo Kulebele funerals; Bolpe, Sumo, Kolia, Kanono and Djemtana could be counted on to perform at Korhogo Kulebele funerals as well as the Korhogo Kulebele Poro. At important funerals one Fonombele and at least two *senambele* Poro would also participate. Thus, the absence or presence of the Danebolo Kulebele Poro would neither add nor detract from a Korhogo Kulebele funeral. Also, funeral gifts of cloth, money, food and livestock that pass from guests to hosts would not be major contributions to Korhogo Kulebele funerals from Danebolo Kulebele who number few and are generally poverty stricken. Finally, Danebolo Kulebele are not a source of carvings for Korhogo Kulebele with the exception of helmet masks carved by the elder who is now the Danebolo Kulebele *kafu*. However, he is not the only source of helmet masks although, because of his extreme poverty and constant need for immediate cash to feed his remaining wife and her children, he is forced to sell his work for one-third the price other carvers realize. By absorbing the Danebolo Kulebele into his own politico-economic system the Korhogo Kulebele *kafu* would have had access to increased manpower and economic benefits, but their determination to remain autonomous resulted in his attempts to force them to comply with his wishes by withholding economic and ritual assistance.

Because of their few numbers and poverty, Danebolo Kulebele are in a difficult position. Only three of them have ever achieved wealth to any degree. One man has worked at the museum in Abidjan since 1960, rarely visits Korhogo and has married a Baule woman; his contributions to his *narigba7a* are virtually nonexistent. Another man is the new Danebolo Kulebele *kafu* who is reported to have been very wealthy in the past but excessive medical expenses paid to traditional healers after he was seriously injured in a bush taxi accident many years ago, plus his wife's depredations noted above, resulted in impoverishment that he has never been able to overcome. Indeed, as an elder in his mid- or late-60's, he should ideally be retired from carving, but prior to his ascension to *kafu* he had no *pibele* to aide in his support. He has one remaining brother, also in his 60's, in very poor health, unproductive and an alcoholic—one of three alcoholic Kulebele—and his oldest child, a son, is only in his mid-teens. This *kafu* and his brother are two of the three adult Kulebele males still living in mud-brick and thatch huts in Korhogo, which is an indication of their poverty.

The remaining wealthy Danebolo Guleo is the acting-*kafu* mentioned above. It was his largess that made an appropriate funeral possible for the Danebolo Kulebele *kafu* in 1975, although as *naro* of the deceased *kafu* he was obliged to provide a fine funeral. Because of kinship alliances with Sumo and Djemtana Kulebele, both of their Poro performed at the funeral, as well as that of Danebolo. Fonombele and two *senambele* Poro orchestras and *senambele* Poro maskers also performed. Thus, the funeral was attended by many Poro and there were gifts of cloth, money and food, but the amounts of the gifts were not as spectacular as those given at Korhogo Kulebele funerals nor at the funerals of wealthy Senufo chiefs. Had the Korhogo Kulebele participated, the gifts would probably have been nearly doubled.

Although they are few in numbers and generally poor, no apparent advantage would accrue to the Danebolo Kulebele by becoming *pibele* of the Korhogo Kulebele *kafu.* Indeed, as members of his Poro, initiation fees and initiate manpower would flow from their group to that of their new *kafu.* Also, their political organization and status would be directly subordinate to Korhogo Kulebele. However, in spite of their attempts to remain independent, future autonomy is uncertain. New rural Kulebele immigrants who will be initiated into Kulebele Poro in Korhogo are now "trapped" by the Korhogo Kulebele *kafu,* and Danebolo

Kulebele must depend upon their own kinship ties for new initiates. It appears that the Danebolo Kulebele political organization and Poro will ultimately collapse from lack of personnel, which will result in their eventual subordination to the Korhogo Kulebele *kafu*.

Political Organization and Islam

Many *senambele* chiefs are not only Poro elders but are also Muslims. The earliest conversion of a *senambele* chief in Korhogo occurred in the late 19th century when a son of Zokenya, *senambele* chief of Korhogo, was sent to Sikasso, Mali, as a hostage to live in the court of Babemba, a Muslim. When Zokenya died, Gbon, backed by Babemba's troops, returned to Korhogo in 1892 and claimed his father's position as chief. Gbon's ascension to chieftainship was unique in that his claim was based upon patrilineal descent, whereas matrilineal succession had previously been the rule. Subsequently, in Korhogo, *senambele* political rights were inherited through the patriline and conversion to Islam was usual. However, among *senambele*, becoming Muslim does not preclude participation in Poro; all elder Muslim *senambele* are still active as Poro elders, attend Poro funerals regardless of which Poro are performing, share in Poro initiation fees and monies collected at funerals, and are given Poro funerals when they die. Thus, among *senambele*, Poro participation and being a Muslim are not mutually exclusive categories.

There are less than a dozen Kulebele converts to Islam, all of whom, with the exception of one man, converted to Islam after completing their Poro initiation and achieving the status of elder. Kulebele converts who are *pibele* of the Korhogo Kulebele *kafu*, which includes his oldest son and all of his *narobele*, participate only marginally in Poro. They provide money for Poro funeral expenses and they attend the public presentation of funeral cloths, which is an important part of every funeral, and sometimes attend Kulebele Poro mask performances. However, they do not enter the Kulebele *sinzang* in Korhogo and they avoid contact with all non-Kulebele Poro and Poro performances, which means they do not participate in Kulebele funerals when non-Kulebele Poro perform.[41] Neither do they learn the secrets of the Kafigelejo, a powerful and greatly feared Kulebele "fetish"

57

through which the initiated can divine and implement negative supernatural sanctions against others.[42]

A very important function of *narigbafobele* and *kafubele* is the protection of their *pibele* from supernaturally caused disasters, such as illness, barrenness and death, which often result from the magical manipulations of others. The machinations of the Nafoun Kulebele Poro are an example of the mischief that can be perpetrated through supernatural powers. The Korhogo Kulebele *kafu* consulted his Kafigelejo to divine the source of the dancers' convulsions and it was medicine provided by the *kafu* that cured the convulsions. All Kulebele chiefs are recognized—and feared—as possessing great supernatural powers as a result of their control of Kafigelejo.

As discussed above, among Kulebele, political position is inherited through the *narigba7a;* thus the *narobele* of the current Korhogo Kulebele *kafu* are next in line of succession upon the demise of the *kafu.* However, they are Muslims, participate only marginally in Kulebele Poro and avoid contact with the Kafigelejo. As *kafu,* none would be able to fulfill all of the functions traditionally associated with Kulebele chiefs. He would not be able to perform important Poro duties, such as consulting the Kafigelejo about propitious days for various Poro activities or funerals. He would not enter the *sinzang* where many Poro rituals and ceremonies occur and the absence of the *narigbafolo* at these ceremonies has no precedent. He would be unable to coordinate the activities of his Poro with non-Kulebele Poro. Neither could he fulfill all of the duties incumbent upon funeral hosts when non-Kulebele Poro participate at Kulebele funerals. Finally, he would be unable to fulfill his duties as protector of his *pibele* because he avoids the Kafigelejo and has not learned the techniques for activating and controlling its powers. His political position would not be backed by Poro or the Kafigelejo, both of which are important sources of ritual and political validation.

The *narobele* of the present *kafu* claim that they are next in line of succession to the chieftainship of the Korhogo Kulebele. However, agnatic descendents of the *kafu* state that one of his "sons" *(nojabele)* will assume leadership of the Poro and responsibility for Kafigelejo-related matters. The *kafu* overtly favors two sons who are brothers and whose mother "has the chief's ear." The elder brother is an initiate in a *senambele* Poro and has completed all three Kulebele Poro grades. These two brothers assist their aged father with his tourist art market dealings and share disproportionately, relative to his other sons, in his real-estate holdings. It is probable that the oldest son will inherit his father's ritual and protective roles. Thus, ritual and secular rights and obligations will be invested in two individuals—a new way of delegating political roles in Kulebele experience.

Kulebele political organization and Poro are both integral to the *narigba7a*. The larger the Poro membership, the more status accrues to the *narigba7a* and the *narigbafolo,* but it is also crucial that there be a sufficient number of Poro initiates to insure the performance of prescribed funeral rites and to host at funerals. Although the *narigba7a* provides the core membership of its Poro, other social alliances are also a means of recruiting Poro initiates. Competition between *kafubele* for initiates into their Poro has been exacerbated by the desire to participate in the tourist art market. Many Kulebele now migrate to Korhogo to participate in this market and in the Danebolo case, an entire group and their *kafu* migrated to Korhogo for this reason. The result has been stiff competition between *kafubele* and conflict between Kulebele groups as each attempts to enhance its politico-economic position. Thus, decisions are made upon the basis of economic advantage in the tourist art market and political advantage which result in increased Poro manpower and initiation fees and extended political suzerainty. Islam has also contributed to changing political policies. Upon the demise of their *kafu,* who is in his late eighties, Korhogo Kulebele will be faced with coping with a new system of politico-ritual organization, the success of which is yet to be assured.

4

Traditional
Artists and Tourist Art

Traditionally, Kulebele were articulated into Senufo society as strangers who perceived themselves primarily as carvers and secondarily as farmers. In fact, however, few men were able to sustain themselves solely by carving and most farmed as well as carved. Indeed, some Kulebele never became adept at carving and depended for subsistence on farming alone augmented by keeping livestock and trading. Prepubertal boys helped women in the fields and tended small livestock, while teenage boys worked in the fields and tended cattle for their father or *sheleo*. Learning to carve was a secondary occupation and only those who sought to pursue carving as a primary occupation learned to carve all the items in the Kulebele repertoire. A list of items carved by Kulebele is given in Table 2, some of which are illustrated in plates 9 through 14. Most Kulebele specialized in a few items and sometimes only one. Thus, the current chief of Kanono 1 carves only mortars and pestles and one of the Kulebele in Korhogo carves only stools. A Bolpe carver living in the Dikodougou area carves mortars and pestles and one model of a face mask for the tourist art market. Himmelheber (1960:114) reports that Kulebele villages have specific specialties and that Kanono Kulebele must go to Korhogo Kulebele for masks for traditional use. In fact, the men from Kanono who do know how to carve masks were in residence in Korhogo in order to exploit the tourist art market in 1973, having moved there some years earlier. Korhogo residence does not make Korhogo-ites of them: they are still considered to be Kanono-ites. These men learned to carve masks from Kulebele living in Korhogo. Specialization is the result of opportunity and interest. A carver learns to make those objects which others in the village carve, but must often migrate in order to study with a master carver and expand his repertoire: there are no taboos in learning to carve particular items. Not all Kulebele are known as carvers and some do not carve at all. Of those that do, many are specialized in carving the more mundane everyday objects used within the household for which there is a more regular demand and a steadier market than that for ritual paraphernalia.

Table 2
Objects Carved by Kulebele

Household Items:	Ritual Paraphernalia:
mortars and pestles	staffs
bowls	stools
spoons	drums
food stirrers (2 types)	flutes
stools	guitar bridges
chairs	helmet masks (several categories)
cosmetic jars	face masks (several categories)
	statues
Miscellaneous:	
heddle pulleys	
shuttles	Prestige Items:
knives, adzes	chief's chairs
hoe handles	doors
oars	
beer measures	

Learning to Carve

Boys learn to carve by observing their elders and copying their technique. Plates 5 through 8 illustrate carving tools and how they are held. Until a boy is 12 or 13 years old, little attempt is made to instruct him. A child is told to help in the fields, or with livestock, or to run errands, but he is not told to practice carving. A boy's first efforts at carving begin at about five years of age when his attempts at carving are incorporated into his play. His first tools are usually old, dull adzes cast aside by older carvers though, rarely, a boy may be provided with a set of scaled-down tools. Attempts by the child to use larger, heavier and sharper adzes are quickly stopped. The child is not guided in his efforts except by harsh verbal commands should he handle an adze in a manner that threatens injury to himself.[43] The first wood a boy practices on is that of the bombax tree (*Celiba pertandra Gaertn* and *Bombax brevicuspe Sprague*), since it is soft and easier to manage than harder woods. Children are neither encouraged to carve nor discouraged. By the time the boy is eight to ten years old, he is beginning to experiment with old, rusty carving knives. As with adzes, there is no direct instruction on how to handle the knife unless the child handles it in such a way as to constitute a potential danger to himself.

The child learns by copying those immediately older and more experienced than himself. While small boys may be found carving in their father's company, it is more usual that they work with their age mates. In the Korhogo Kulebele chief's *ka7a*, which is comprised of 33 males from five years of age and up, the males work in eight basic work-groups. One work-group is comprised of prepubertal and pubertal boys, another of teenagers; two groups consist of young men in their early twenties and two are made up of middle-aged men; one group consists of a man and his sons, and one is comprised of two elder brothers and an eldest son. Thus, work-groups are more likely to segregate themselves according to age than by kinship until men become older. As the skills of the individual surpass those generally attained by others of his work-group, he aligns himself with the next advanced work-group until he has reached full maturity, at which point he will generally be found in the company of full brothers. Diagram 11 illustrates the working arrangements of Kulebele living in Quartier Koko.

When a boy reaches a point in his carving where he is unable to proceed further without instruction, his father shows him how to proceed by example. For instance, a prepubertal boy's statues were consistently lopsided. His father unobtrusively re-dressed several pieces of wood the boy had prepared for carving. The problem lay in careless preparation of the stock, which the father quickly rectified. The boy followed his father's example and the problem was solved. As a boy becomes more competent in his carving, he seeks to work with carvers who can increase his knowledge until he has reached the point where control of his

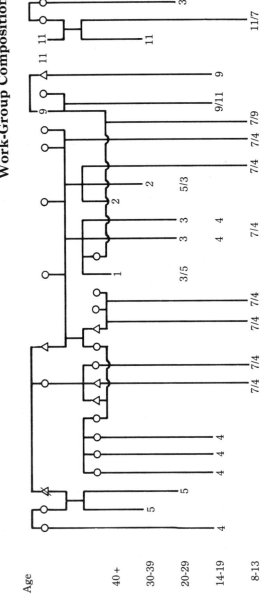

Diagram 11
Work-Group Composition

Numerals are work-group designations: two numerals indicate participation in two work-groups.

Free-floating numbers refer to distant kin or *nubombele.*

64

tools is precise, but he still lacks experience in carving difficult items such as helmet masks, face masks and large statues. It is at this point in his carving career that he seeks out a master carver who may or may not be a kinsman. A carver working under a master carver also learns by example. He observes what is being done and copies the adze strokes and progress of the work of his *tamofo* (one who knows).

The *tamofo* is obliged to accept any Kulebele who chooses to work with him. Kulebele feel that they have an obligation to help one another with their carving. The length of apprenticeship is determined by the *barapipiu* (small-work child, i.e., apprentice) who works under the tutelage of the *tamofo* as long as the *barapipiu* desires. The relationship cannot be terminated by the *tamofo*. The *tamofo* does not charge a fee for his teaching, but the *barapipiu* gives him occasional gifts of kola and performs chores and runs errands for him. As the work of the *barapipiu* progresses, he is given more difficult carving tasks until he feels he has learned what he sought to master. The formal reciprocal aspects of the *tamofo/barapipiu* relationship, namely, teaching/gift-giving and performing chores are then terminated, though the social relationship persists and is manifested by the *barapipiu* calling on and greeting his *tamofo* and performing occasional small chores for him.

The Tourist Art Market

Kulebele have always exploited the carving market available to them and have gone to great lengths to protect their exclusivity as carvers, which will be discussed in Chapter 6. While they enjoy a special relationship with their farmer hosts who provide them with food and housing, they also receive cowries and/or francs for the items they produce.[44] Kulebele, then, have long been accustomed to producing for strangers, i.e., people belonging to groups other than their own. Not only do they carve for Senufo but also for non-Senufo, e.g., Hausa and Dyula, for whom they produce drums, and for many other ethnic groups for whom they produce mortars and pestles and other household utensils. Dealings with Senegalese, Hausa and white buyers of masks and statues have been subsumed into an already extant system of receiving payment for goods produced and, in fact, have resulted in payment in francs which were needed and sought after for paying taxes and buying European manufactured goods.

The tourist art market began for Kulebele when they were forced to carve for French administrators in the early twentieth century. Remuneration to any degree was not realized until the 1940's and in the following twenty years, tourist art market demands reached the point where all eastern Kulebele were being affected by it directly or indirectly. Men were either involved in producing carvings for the tourist art market or were receiving income from sons, sons-in-law and *narobele* who were producing for it. Migration patterns were affected as master carvers migrated to take advantage of the new market and apprentices sought to follow in order to learn the techniques for producing masks and statues for the tourist art market. Younger men in the East who had only known how to carve utilitarian items sought to master the technique for carving at least one model of mask for the tourist market. The opportunity presented by the tourist market stimulated Kulebele to carve who would not ordinarily be doing so in the traditional context. Indeed, successful farming Kulebele gave up farming to become mediocre and poor carvers.

Traditional and Tourist Carvers

Almost all Kulebele who carve, carve for the tourist art market, although not all carving Kulebele produce for the traditional market. Kulebele group carvers into three basic categories, the first of which consists of "hack" carvers (Cordwell 1970:47) who would not be carving or would be limited to household-type items in the traditional market. The second category consists of carvers who are adequate but timid craftsmen in terms of the range of items they carve. The third category includes carvers with a command of a wide repertoire of masks, statues and chairs.

Hack carvers and teenagers are responsible for the bulk of poor quality items found in the tourist art market. Examples of their work are illustrated in plate 13. The output of this category of carver is described by Graburn (1976b:7) as "souvenir arts" in which "the standards and aesthetic values of the producer group as well as the market . . . are often compromised by needs of fast production and a cheap price." Often carvers in this category have mastered the technique for carving only one model of face mask or statue. The masks they produce are not and would not be used in the traditional context; they are crudely done and exhibit poor craftsmanship. Statues of *ndebele* (bush spirits) produced by this group could be used traditionally since they are not publicly displayed and the critical facilities of a Poro are not applied to them as is the case with Poro masks.[45] However, many of these men are so specialized they do not know how to carve statues and should the opportunity present itself, they would pass the commission on to a carver who does.

Carvers such as these are perceived in two different lights by other Kulebele. Kulebele who are involved in the tourist art market as dealers regard them as sources of carvings for which there is a ready market; their products are needed and their carvings bought no matter how crudely executed. However, the poorest of these poor carvers receives even less for his efforts than his colleagues. Thus it behooves all to attain at least a minimal degree of excellence. Masks of this quality can be produced at the rate of one mask per day.[46]

Most of the carvers of this ilk are found in the Dikodougou area or western Kulebeleland, though carvers in the West do not have the expertise to manufacture masks so rapidly and are just as likely to carve statues with which they have had more practice. The efforts of western carvers are not as severely criticized by fine carvers: westerners are recognized as not having the experience nor *tamofo* that good quality work requires. Indeed, some adult western men, who migrated to Korhogo to carve for the tourist art market, did not know how to carve before their arrival in Korhogo and were taught to carve by Kulebele in Korhogo.

Dikodougou area carvers, many of whom are from Sumo, are harshly criticized by good carvers for their hasty and ill-conceived work and the cheap prices their efforts command. They are accused of "breaking" the market in terms of esthetics and price. Esthetically, the products of these carvers are regarded as lacking merit. Indeed, they are hardly considered at all other than as something tourists buy and are of interest only as income-producing items. On the other hand, poor quality work is perceived as a threat to undermining the price of better quality work and better carvers fear that foreign buyers will not be able to discern between good carving and poor, and thereby expect to pay lower prices for better work.

Teenagers' carving does not elicit the same kinds of responses. Since they are *barapipibele,* their work cannot be compared critically to that of adults, for their errors result from the learning process rather than hasty execution.

The craftsmanship of objects produced by the second category of carvers is generally high in quality but lacking in originality. These carvers often copy traditional Senufo-type masks and statutes. They use harder woods than teenagers and hack carvers and pay careful attention to detail. Three dimensions are fully exploited and their work is carefully symmetrical, both of which are Kulebele esthetic virtues. Their work is appreciated but elicits little comment for they are content to reproduce the same forms month after month, year after year. Often their repertoire is limited to a half dozen or fewer items and new, innovative or difficult to carve objects are not expected of them. They produce for the traditional market, but since their repertoire is often foreign to traditional usage there is little demand for their work except within the context of the tourist art market. They receive three to five times higher prices for their tourist market masks than do carvers in the first category. Most carvers of this type are to be found in Korhogo. Examples of their work can be seen in plate 13.

The third category carvers produce the bulk of traditional Poro paraphernalia and the most expensive tourist art items. The work of these carvers would be categorized as "commercial fine art," according to Graburn's (1976b:7) typology, for they "adhere to the high standards and aesthetic values of the producer groups as well as the market. . ." They generally work within the traditional context rather than being stimulated by imported ideas. They are slow workers, sometimes taking a week to complete a mask and three weeks or longer to complete a giant hornbill. Because they produce a wide range of items and are often engaged in producing objects that are difficult and not ordinarily carved, their work elicits a great deal of interest and admiration. Examples of their work are illustrated in plates 9 through 12. These carvers are believed to have been endowed with special "good luck" *(kacana)* by Kolocelo, the supreme diety and creation god, which accounts for their outstanding ability. These are the Kulebele who are sought out as *tamofo* and by Poro to produce ritual masks and statues. Because of the demand for their work, they can be and are discriminating about the commissions they accept. The attitude of these carvers towards first category carvers is much the same as Gola carvers' attitude towards carpenters, who are perceived as a threat to the "standards of the craft" of woodcarving (d'Azevedo 1970:52).

In view of the above clarification of the types of carvers found among the Kulebele and because of their varying activities, it is clear that not all carvers have been affected by the presence of the tourist market in such a way that quantity has affected quality. Carvers of the first category produce quantities of inferior quality carvings for the tourist art market, which provides them with the only opportunity they have to carve. Within the traditional context they would be producing only utilitarian items or not carving at all. On the other hand, exploitation of a carving market, be it traditional or European, is the *modus operandi* of the Kulebele. Exploitation of the tourist art market is an expected course of events whether by top-quality carvers or hack artists.

Carvers of the third category have been positively affected by the tourist market. Traditionally they would have had less opportunity to carve than today. Like Kwahu potters (Sieber 1972:179) and Fang carvers (Fernandez 1973:199) who may be commissioned to execute but a few objects in a year or a lifetime, most Kulebele were not engaged in carving full-time. The tourist market has allowed them to work throughout the year. Thus, carvers get more practice carving now than in the past. Further, the diverse demands of the tourist market require that top carvers be constantly expanding their repertoire which they have developed on traditional motifs and new techniques are being developed that are unknown to older and rural carvers. Incising is an example of the expansion of technique made possible by constant opportunity to carve and practice with carving tools. Most top-quality work is currently going into private collections and has not yet reached the attention of museums, nor has it been published.

Traders and Rewards

Himmelheber (1963:88) states:
> A Senufo artist remains anonymous his life long . . . consider what this must mean for the true artist. His inspiration, his efforts, his skill will not be rewarded by the applause of his public, for the public does not know him. All the stimulus which ambition furnishes to the artist does not become effective in Senufo art . . . yet Senufo art reaches the highest levels.

The assumption in the above quotation appears to be that only the consuming public rewards the artist with recognition, which is not the case. Kulebele receive recognition from colleagues and, since the tourist art market has developed, from dealers. Indeed, a man's ability determines price which, in turn, determines the kind of trader that deals with him and the manner in which he sells his work. First and second category carvers work in anticipation of sales and sell primarily to Kulebele who have become tourist market dealers. Third category carvers work on selected commissions only and sell to higher paying foreign dealers who are usually Senegalese, Hausa and French. There is little prestige to be gained by mass-producing carvings in anticipation of sales to Kulebele dealers who pay low prices, but there is much prestige to be gained by working on commission for discriminating dealers who are willing to pay well for the work they buy. Thus a carver's status in the community is enhanced not only by the kinds of items he produces, but also by the sector of the market he sells to, the manner of production and the price received.[47]

Dealers are adamant and firm in their appraisal and pay accordingly. Once a carver's reputation has been established on the basis of quality, he deals with those traders who are willing and able to pay his price. All dealers carry *nyama-nyama* (junk, odds and ends) but some deal in it exclusively. These are the dealers who are either just beginning in business or who have been unsuccessful. They are men who do not have access to cash to pay for top quality work. The exception to this general rule are Kulebele who have become traders. Kulebele dealers draw on kinship relations and mutual "Kulebeleness" to exploit the output of first category carvers. They function as middlemen between these carvers and foreign dealers. Selling to Kulebele does not confer prestige upon the carver for they have a general reputation for paying poorly and short-changing.

Traders are also responsible for the dissemination of innovations. A carving by a master carver will often be taken to a second category carver to copy provided that the item is not too complex. Innovations drift from master carver to second category and hack carvers; they rarely drift the other way.

Dealers encourage, present gifts to and make social calls on the carvers they deal with, as well as extend invitations to them to share food. One dealer begins his rounds every morning at six, calling on all the carvers who carve for him, as well as those he hopes will find time to carve for him in the future. His daily calls are generally finished by late morning. This dealer presents small gifts of money to his carvers and their wives and children, and items of clothing to the top carvers who carve for him. He also invites carvers to share meals with him at which he provides an abundance of meat which is a highly valued and prestigious food. Further, he pays partially in advance and makes loans to favored carvers. By creating a multiplex bond with his carvers, he can expect rapid completion of his orders and favored treatment from those he commissions. "I'll finish Aladijen's work first; he's always very nice to me and gives me lots of presents," was the comment made by a master carver who was being pressured by Aladijen and another trader to complete each one's work first.

This kind of relationship is not needed with first category carvers whose work is stereotyped and limited. The volume of their work guarantees that it will always be readily available. What is of more concern to traders dealing with better merchandise is that the number of master carvers, who do not produce in high volume quantities and whose time is contracted for weeks in advance, is limited. A top carver usually has several weeks' and sometimes months' work contracted for in advance. If a dealer has a rush job and has not established multiplex bonds with his carvers, he may be forced to second category carvers to fulfill the job.

Thus, it is clear that carvers do have an active and interested audience, for not only do their colleagues take an interest in their work, but traders too, play an important role as critics. Indeed, traders are considered more knowledgeable about the carvers' craft, its limitations and possibilities, changing styles and esthetics, than the European tourists who occasionally visit at the carvers' work area. The latter inevitably choose a low quality piece of work because of its price and its crudeness, which are considered by them to be "typique d'Afrique."

For the Kulebele, learning to carve is an endeavor predicated on personal preference and ability. The development of the tourist art market has created a market for inferior quality merchandise that is being supplied by men who would not be carving masks and statues in the traditional context. Master carvers, however, continue to produce high quality items that are admired by both their fellow carvers and traders. The opportunity to carve full-time as opposed to part-time, which was the case before the advent of the tourist market, has generally allowed carvers to become more adept at their craft. Skill in carving is appreciated and encouraged by tourist market dealers who reward top carvers with admiration and benefits not extended to less talented carvers.

Plate 1   Kulebele holdings in Quartier Koko, Korhogo

Plate 2   Tyoronyaradougou market on a major market day

Plate 3 Kulebele work area in Quartier Kok

Plate 4 Kulebele houses in Quartier Kok

Plate 5 Carving knives

Plate 6 Using a carving knife

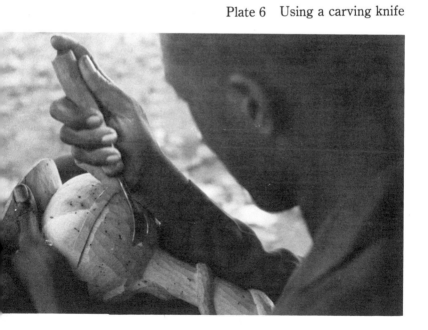

Plate 7 Carving adzes

Plate 8 Using a carving adze

Plate 9 Wanugu

Plate 10 *Kpelie* by Ngolo
Coulibaly (Kolia) 1976

Plate 11 *Kpelie* by Liyerege
(Dabakaha) early 1940's

77

Plate 12   Wanugı

Plates 13 and 14   Tourist art market mask

Plate 15   Kulebele houses in Sumo

Plate 16   Kulebele cattle at Sumo

79

Plate 17   Kulebele rental units in Korhogo

Plate 18   Staining mass-produced tourist art market mask

5

Migration

Traditionally, the Kulebele population in any given settlement was small and comparatively stable, though membership was constantly changing. As men became adept as carvers, it was necessary that they migrate in order to find work. These migrations were spontaneous and self-imposed though stimulated by the need to seek new markets for their production.

The Kulebele dispersed southward from Mali. As noted above, at least one segment of Kulebele originated in Segou approximately 190 years ago when Kulebele migrated to San (see Map 2). From San, subsequent precolonial migrations resulted in the Kulebele populations at Tiogo.[48] Kulebele in Kouto have no tradition of origins other than that they emigrated from Mali. Kouto Kuelebele subsequently provided the nucleus for Kulebele populations in Dabakaha, Kolia and Zanguinasso. Kolia was also settled by Kulebele from Vonoloho, where there are no longer Kulebele, and Zanguinasso received Kulebele from Bolpe. The origins of the Ouezoumon Kulebele are vague: their tradition indicates that they migrated from "behind" *(kado)* Kouto.[49]

In the East, Bolpe is considered to be the oldest Kulebele village and the dispersal point from which all other eastern Kulebele villages were populated. Bolpe Kulebele maintain they emigrated from Mali and have been in Bolpe since it was founded. Subsequent migrations from Bolpe resulted in Kulebele becoming established in Kposulugo, Kanono, Sumo, Djemtana, Danebolo, Korhogo and Zanguinasso. From Sumo, Kuelebele continued their southward drift to Nafoun. All of these migrations occurred before the Samori wars in the area, which began in the early 1880's.[50]

Kulebele Migration Routes

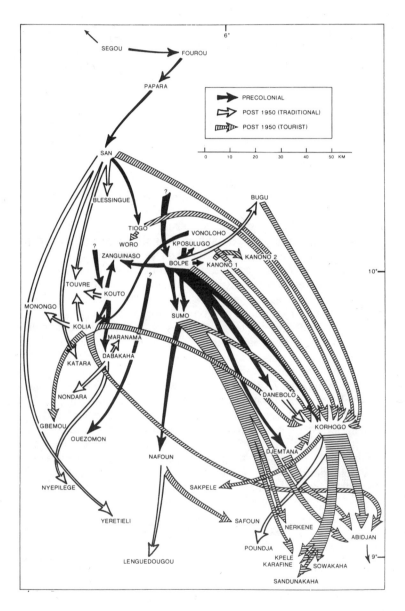

While pre-colonial migrations were voluntary, many migrations that occurred during the colonial period were undertaken unwillingly. Kulebele were sent to Bouaké as impressed labor to carve for colonial administrators, and talented carvers were sent from *en brousse* to Boundiali and to Korhogo, which were administrative posts. Less talented or unrecognized carvers were sent to work on colonial farms, and Kulebele were used for building and repairing bridges because of their familiarity with woodworking techniques, which was recognized by the colonialist.[51] Carvers in Kolia and Dabakaha were carving for the French as forced laborers before 1913. The French administrative post in the Boundiali area was originally established at Tombougou, five kilometers north of Boundiali, in 1897 (Rapport des Tournées 1909). It was moved to Boundiali in 1913 (Angouvant 1913). The present *kafu* of the Kolia Kulebele carved for the French when they were still at Tombougou, as did Kulebele in Dabakaha. Indeed, Dabakaha Kulebele state that the doors to the French quarters in Tombougou were carved in bas-relief by them.

Kulebele received food, sometimes housing and cast-off clothing, but were rarely given money for their efforts. One carver from Boundiali, after carving under French impressment in Boundiali for several years, was sent to France to carve where he remained for "three years," thence to Odienné for "five years" and finally was allowed to settle in Ouezoumon where he had kinsmen. After the policy of forced labor was ended in 1946, Kulebele began realizing an income from the carvings they produced for the French; the demand for carvings increased and Kulebele were stimulated to migrate in order to tap the new and economically productive market. This trend continues and is the major stimulus for migration today as it was during pre-colonial times.

Traditional Migration[52]

Whereas customers traditionally travelled to Kulebele settlements to order ritual and household items, and household objects were carved in anticipation of sales in nearby markets or from the carver's home, the majority of Kulebele engaged in carving sought to increase their income by migrating. Kulebele men sought host-villages[53] in which they would settle for three to five years while Kulebele women moved regularly from village to village as itinerant calabash menders until the birth of their first child. Migrant Kulebele families travelled as far as 90 kilometers, and sometimes more, in pursuit of work as carvers. In spite of the distances involved, Kulebele kept in close contact with one another. Carvers and their dependents travelled from host-villages to Kulebele villages and from one Kulebele village to another to participate in Poro activities, attend funerals, tend to livestock investments and visit kinsmen. Wives and their children were sent to the wife's village of origin in order to maintain *narigba7a* ties.

Men who were members of the *narigba7a* which provided the *kafu* of a Kulebele village and were in line to become *kafu* would migrate temporarily, for their political destinies were in their natal village or that of their mother's brother. Men who were not in line for a chieftainship and who were dedicated to carving rather than farming would be more likely to migrate permanently with other men with the same propensities who were in a similar political situation. These men had fewer commitments in terms of political responsibilities and opportunities in their natal villages and were freer and more prone to emigration than men in the chiefly line. Further, since they had few political prerogatives in their village of origin, they had little to lose by migrating permanently and, often, much to gain. As younger income-producing men,[54] they were obliged to provide for older non-income-producing members of their group and the more wealth they generated, the more demands were made. By migrating they were more easily able to conceal the extent of their wealth and avoid having to share it with kinsmen. This situation still exists in the western area which has been little affected by the tourist art market. As one English-speaking Guleo states: "It is impossible to guard money when you live in the same village as your relatives. That is why men migrate." Elder men in the West complain bitterly about their younger men migrating, even though the young men are often migrating within the traditional context rather than seeking to exploit the tourist art market. Examples of expenditures to elders include meat, ingyams and grains for elder male and female kinsmen who no longer work in the fields; clothing, medicines and fees in the form of cowries and food for diviners and medicine men; and livestock and funeral cloths for funerals.

Permanent migration did not preclude marriage because Kulebele men encounter little resistance to their contracting exogamous marriages. Nor did permanent migration preclude the performance of funeral rites necessary to send one's *pil* to the village-of-the-dead. All Kulebele are entitled to funeral rites performed by Kulebele appropriate to their age and Poro standing. Even children are given funeral rites, though nothing as elaborate as those of full-fledged Poro members. A carver of high Poro rank, who was able to accumulate wealth because of the demand for his carvings, was in a position to rely less and less on fees collected at Kulebele funerals and from Kulebele Poro initiation fees to supplement his income. If he wished, he could join a Poro in the village to which he had migrated and become a participating member which included having a share in Poro collections and fees. Migrating Kulebele who established themselves permanently in a host-village might establish their own Poro in time and realize a political presence they could never attain in their natal village.

Factors other than political considerations and economic goals also influenced migration patterns, e.g., age, reputation and ability as a carver, and kinship and friendship networks. Men less than 25 years of age rarely migrated as independent agents; rather they would migrate as part of the entourage of a more mature carver to whom they were *barapipibele.*[55]

A Guleo whose work was admired was sought out individually. Such a man became more in demand that his less talented kinsmen, received more invitations to reside in host-villages and had better opportunity to accumulate wealth which was ultimately invested in livestock. There was a direct relationship between ability and reputation as a carver and wealth, which influenced the age at which a carver would retire from migrating if, indeed, his migrations were temporary ones.

The number of dependents a carver had to maintain and their income-producing abilities were also relevant factors; as long as all of his children were young and unproductive, he continued to migrate. Economically independent sons supplemented their father's economic resources and daughters were given in marriage to older, wealthy carvers who could be called upon to donate cowries, foodstuffs and livestock to their fathers-in-law. Only very poor carvers continued to migrate past their mid-forties. They were carvers who did not have enough wealth to sustain them until they could look to their children for support. They were Kulebele who had not been able to make economically advantageous marriages for their daughters or whose sons lacked the resources to contribute to their support.

Migrating carvers took their younger sons and sisters' sons with them. If a man were a carver of renown, the younger men's proximity to him gave them an advantage over men attached to lesser-known carvers, though this advantage became inoperative if a young man was slovenly or uninspired in his work. For example Jepe, a widely known and respected carver, attracts more work than he can manage, both traditional and for the tourist market. His son, who is in his 30's, is given much of the excess work. Indeed, he does a great deal of Jepe's work, for which he is beginning to receive recognition from African and French dealers as well as from various Poro. Traders deal with the son directly now and Poro initiates know that a commission to Jepe may be executed by his son, which is agreeable to them because of the excellence of the son's work. On the other hand, Jepe's wife's sister's son also resides with him. The wife's kinsman is a competent but unoriginal carver who is satisfied to carve the items in his limited repertoire time and again. Jepe does not give excess commissions to this man though he and his son receive more requests for work than they can execute. Neither is Jepe criticized for not giving work to his wife's kinsman, nor does the kinsman expect that he should in spite of the fact that the kinsman is a dependent of Jepe. Both Jepe and the kinsman are aware of the latter's limitations.

Migration could be initiated in three ways: 1) a farmer *kafu* of an established village might seek out a specific carver of renowned reputation and invite him to reside with him and to carve for him and his *pibele*. 2) A man might invite a Guleo to migrate with him to establish a new village. 3) An unsolicited carver could seek a host-village. In the first two types of migration, *kafubele* encourage the migration and in the latter, the carver initiates the migration. In all cases the relationship of carver as *nubu* with a *jatugu* was the same; he and his dependents were provided with housing and food and given land use-rights and the carver was given an abundance of cowrie shells and livestock for the items he carved. If the migration was a temporary one, the carver and his dependents would remain from three to five years. A continuing influx of commissions in a host-village was encouragement for Kulebele to continue returning to the village as temporary migrants or to remain in the village as permanent settlers. As migrating Kulebele converged on a host-village, the migrant population increased, kinship and social networks became established and Kulebele would become permanently ensconced. Two generations of children born in a host-village were sufficient to bestow permanent status as a Kulebele settlement upon a host-village. It was by this process that pre-colonial migrations from Bolpe resulted in the establishment of new Kulebele settlements.

Villages that attracted several Kulebele as permanent residents were either large or located in an area with a dense distribution of villages; these characteristics guaranteed that commissions would continue indefinitely. Korhogo, at the beginning of the twentieth century, had a population of 3,600 (Delafosse 1908a) and Kolia, Koute and Zanguinasso had populations in excess of 1,000 (Rapport Mensuels 1906). Bolpe was the administrative center of a traditional kingdom around which were scattered, but dense, populations. Djemtana and Danebolo were small villages but were surrounded by many other small villages. Villages that attracted one or two Kulebele in situations of temporary migration were smaller, more isolated and unable to sustain the services of a permanent Kulebele population.

It is clear that Kulebele have been migrating for many generations in order to take advantage of marketing opportunities and that the market influenced whether or not migration to exploit it was permanent or temporary. Large villages, or those in high-density population areas, were more likely to attract permanent migrants than smaller villages or those located in more sparsely settled areas where there was not enough work to warrant Kulebele immigrations.

Contemporary Migration

Kulebele continue to migrate as they did in the past and the migratory drift continues to be predominantly southward. The same factors that stimulated traditional migration—political affiliation, economic goals, age, reputation and ability as a carver, and kinship and friendship networks—still operate but in different ways. Most of the variations can be attributed directly to the tourist art market and the development of Korhogo as an administrative and commercial center.

The impact of European influence and the tourist art market has not been as strongly felt in western Kulebeleland where there is no urban center comparable to Korhogo. Boundiali, the largest urban center in the western area, has a population of less than 5,000 (Ministère du Plan 1973). Most tourist art dealers are based in Korhogo and draw upon the large population of Kulebele in Korhogo and environs for carvings. Thus, the demands of the tourist art market are felt more strongly in the East. Further, the need for cash is less pressing in the West: only Kolia, of all the villages where Kulebele are found in the West, has begun to "modernize." The majority of the population, except in Boundiali, still lives in thatched mud-brick huts, and electricity is not available in most villages. Because there is less urban drain on food resources in the western area than in the East, food is cheaper and land use-rights are easy to obtain. The standard of living is lower and expectations for European-inspired luxuries such as electricity, concrete-block houses, motorbikes, butane lamps, medical care and bell-bottomed trousers are not as acute as in eastern Kulebeleland.

The response of western Kulebele to the lack of interaction with modernization has been to continue in the traditional manner. Farming is as important an activity as carving, and men still migrate to host-villages to carve utilitarian items such as bowls, mortars and pestles and food stirrers as well as Poro equipment. In these migrations to host-villages, the *nubu/jatugu* relationship still prevails and men migrate temporarily or permanently depending upon their *narigba7a* connections. Most of the men who do carve for the tourist market consider it as a supplement to subsistence farming or cash-cropping of cotton, i.e., they carve when they are not engaged in farming. A few young men are beginning to carve full-time, but they are the exception rather than the rule. For example, three young men in their early twenties have migrated from Tiogo to Woro in an attempt to be more easily accessible to tourist art dealers since the road to Tiogo is more or less impassable.

As Korhogo Kulebele become increasingly involved in the tourist art market and control a large portion of it, they are beginning to tap the western area as a source of carvers unsophisticated in terms of prices. Western Kulebele are encouraged by their eastern brethren to remain *en brousse* where they are not exposed to the perils of urban living, i.e., expensive housing, the high cost of food, lack of land for farming and loss of women's labor because of lack of land and their attendant idleness. However, in spite of the negative aspects of urban living that are presented to them, some western Kulebele do migrate to Korhogo to carve for the tourist art market. So much more closely tied are they to farming that those in the West who have migrated to Korhogo have not known how to carve when they arrived: they were taught how to carve by Korhogo Kulebele.

In contrast, eastern Kulebele are totally committed to the tourist market and all are benefiting from it either as carvers, traders, or as elders who are reaping benefits from the tourist art market activities of their *pibele*. While traditional relations still exist between carver and host-village, it is now more common for farmers in need of carved wood objects to seek out Kulebele in their settlements than for Kulebele to migrate for the sole purpose of executing items for traditional use. Thus, traditional items are more often carved at the carver's place of residence than by invitation to host-villages. This is made possible by the greater mobility of the general population by means of public transportation and privately owned motorbikes. However, Kulebele continue to migrate and for some of the same reasons as were traditionally operative.

Political affiliation continues to be an important factor. Men who are politically "well placed," i.e., members of a ruling *narigba7a*, do not migrate permanently. However, their relationship to a *kafu* provides opportunities to exploit long-term, lucrative carving jobs other carvers do not have. The national government recognizes traditional chiefs and takes advantage of their traditional powers to implement national policy when expedient to do so. Thus, when governmental agencies such as the Musée d'Abidjan or the Bureau de Tourism seek carvers, they deal with traditional Kulebele *kafubele* who are anxious that their *pibele* be placed in these jobs. As a result, several kinsmen of the Korhogo and Danebolo Kulebele *kafubele* have taken jobs in Abidjan carving for the museum and at an atélier organized and operated by the Bureau de Tourism in Grand Bassam which is 43 kilometers from Abidjan. The earliest of these coastward migrations occurred in 1961 and men have remained in their jobs for as long as 14 years, but all plan to return to Korhogo and they maintain close ties with kinsmen there. Vacations are spent in Korhogo and visiting kinsmen *en brousse* and wives and children are sent to Korhogo to visit or to live.

However, most migrations are not to urban centers or large villages. Migrations in the East are stimulated by the tourist art market, the center of which is in Korhogo. A shortage of wood in the Bolpe-Kanono-Kposulugo-Sumo area and around Korhogo has resulted in Kulebele migrating to areas where there is an abundance of wood. Lack of wood suitable for carving in the northern areas is due to intensive and extensive agriculture. Vestiges of climax forests found in the North today are sacred forests *(sinzang)* used and protected by Poro. Uncultivated areas are now covered with scrub acacia which is not suitable for carving. There are sufficient desirable trees available for making traditional objects and if carving were restricted to traditional needs, migration to wood sources would not be necessary. However, extant wood sources will not support large groups of Kulebele who are mass-producing carvings. As a result, Kulebele migrate south to villages in the Dikodougou area where a plentiful wood supply exists.

The first migrants to this southern area were Korhogo Kulebele who were employed to carve for the Catholic Church in Dikodougou in 1953. As these carvers established themselves around Dikodougou, other Kulebele, seeking a plentiful source of wood on a main transportation route to Korhogo and close to Korhogo, moved into the area. The result has been significant numbers of Kulebele clustering in small host-villages—as many as nine men and their dependents in a single host-village with a total population of 206. Traditional *nubu/jatugu* relationships do not obtain in such a situation. Kulebele living in these host-villages are there for one purpose only which is to exploit nearby wood sources for tourist art market carving. Farmers are now often involved in cash-crop farming and are not willing to deplete personal resources to support strangers who do not contribute to the village, such as carvers who do not provide carvings for the benefits they receive. Large numbers of stranger Kulebele in a small host-village would constitute a serious drain on village resources. Under these circumstances Kulebele are not provided with food though they are still given housing and land use-rights. Further, if they are commissioned to execute carved wood items for villagers, they are given food during the time they spend carving for villagers and are paid for their work in cowries and/or francs.

Two categories of carvers migrate to the Dikodougou area. The first are 'hack' carvers who cannot command a high enough price for their work to allow them to meet the exigencies of life in Korhogo and whose high volume of work (one mask per day) requires a large supply of accessible wood. Second are men who migrate temporarily to take advantage of less expensive village life in order to accumulate wealth. Living *en brousse* is recognized as a less expensive way of life than that of the towns. Not only is there no rent to pay, but land use-rights can be obtained and women's labor can be exploited in growing subsistence or cash crops.

Young men migrate *en brousse* so as not to be tempted to spend money on women and clothes. Village girls, compared to girls in Korhogo, are considered to be "trop vilaine." They are usually poor and are not able to dress as well as girls in Korhogo and Kulebele girls and do not wear currently fashionable hair styles. Neither are they "propre," i.e., they do not bathe as frequently as Korhogo and Kulebele girls. Further, custom demands that a young man make gifts of money and clothing to girls he desires to sleep with or is sleeping with. Not only are girls in Korhogo considered more attractive than village girls, they also make more demands for money and clothing. Kulebele girls are aware of their young men's greater relative wealth and are equally demanding.

Finally, Kulebele are very clothes-conscious: one's prestige and status are enhanced within the Kulebele context by dressing well and stylishly, be it in western or Muslim style. It is understood that villagers are poor, are not able to dress well and are more tolerant of shabby clothes. They may, in fact, be jealous of chic attire and the wealth it represents and be driven to impose negative supernatural sanctions out of jealousy on the well-dressed individual as a result. Villages, then, are places one migrates to in order to save money and not be distracted by the temptations of urban life.

Men begin migrating in their late teens as soon as they are able to carve statues and masks well enough to sell to traders.[56] Older men continue to migrate until they have saved enough money to buy a motorbike, a building lot, to build a concrete-block house or to accumulate enough capital to invest in wealth-generating investments.

Migration to Korhogo is stimulated by the fact that many of the best carvers reside there. Young boys are often sent from rural areas to live in Korhogo so that they may learn to carve well and young men migrate to Korhogo to learn the finer points of carving and to be exposed to a wider variety of styles and techniques than are found in traditional rural Kulebele settlements. A wide variety of kin links are mobilized in migration to Korhogo, though migrants taking up residence with father's brother account for one-third of the migrant residential patterns.

Migrating to Korhogo as young men or being sent as children for the purpose of learning to carve has been occurring since at least the 1950's. Carvers who were sent to Korhogo as children prefer to remain there, though they temporarily migrate to rural areas when they are young men. Urbanized Kulebele are not content to return permanently to rural areas which lack electricity and have poor water resources and where, because of the smallness of the settlements, their social activities are under the constant scrutiny of their kinsmen. Further, the potential for maximizing wealth by becoming a trader in carvings and investing in improved real estate is severely limited in the rural environment.

Migration has traditionally been the means by which Kulebele have sought to expand marketing opportunities for their wares and they still migrate frequently for the same reasons. However, new factors are apparent as a result of the opportunities presented by tourist art market participation and government regulations concerning land distribution and building codes. The need for men to establish their own *kacolo* at a younger age than in the past, because of building restrictions, makes it necessary that men accumulate enough capital to establish a *kacolo* by the time they are in their thirties if they wish to maintain two or three wives and their children. The tourist market makes this possible but it is necessary that men migrate to avail themselves of an adequate supply of wood, an inexpensive way of life until adequate wealth has been accumulated and also to be within reach of tourist market dealers. Thus, migration continues to be an integral part of Kulebele life; by migrating, men are able to accumulate wealth and to become autonomous.

6

Exploitation
of Supernatural Sanctions

The impact of external influences upon African social systems and its reflection in the arts are often commented upon in the literature.[57] In contrast is the effect of a changing art tradition on social organization and particularly on religious practices. Cook (1970) and Nash (1967) discuss the social implications of artisan activities and fluctuating market opportunities, but the literature does not deal in depth with the effects of tourist art market production on indigenous supernatural beliefs and practices.

Kulebele manipulate supernatural sanctions in conjunction with their carving. Through manipulation of the supernatural Kulebele protect their exclusivity over the art of woodcarving. Without negative sanctions, non-carvers would be free to exploit the carving market, which would result in competition for Kulebele.

African artisan groups—generally called "castes" in the literature—are often described as being "despised," "feared," "mysterious" or occupying a special place in society. Fuga woodworkers of Ethiopia (Shack 1964), əngkyaga blacksmiths on the Nigeria-Cameroon border (Vaughan 1970 and 1973), Dogon blacksmiths (Griaule and Dieterlen 1970:106) and Senufo artisan groups (Knops 1959) are among a few of the peoples in Africa credited with possessing supernatural powers unique to themselves.[58] The Kulebele are another such group; they are feared and despised[59] because they possess and practice supernatural sanctions not available to the rest of the population.

The literature suggests that the attitude of awe directed towards artists by the general population in Africa is related to the powers they possess and forces they control during the process of creation: artists and supernatural powers go hand in glove. The West African artist, according to Knops (1959:89), is a principal traditional agent of magic. The father of Camara Laye, the Guinean writer, was a goldsmith versed in "conjuring evil spirits" (Laye 1954:27) and Soumaoro Kente, king of the Susu, was a blacksmith and "a great sorcerer," whose "fetish had a terrible power" and could "deal a swift death to whoever he pleased" (Niane 1970:38). Zulu blacksmiths dealt with sorcerers and were suspected of being sorcerers themselves (Ritter 1973:44-45). African artists, then, are believed by others to possess supernatural powers. This belief may or may not be shared by the artists themselves. Indeed, Vaughan (1970) states that smiths living amongst the Marghi encourage such beliefs about themselves.

Such is the case with the Kulebele: they control supernatural powers exclusive to themselves. However, these beliefs are not operative unless others believe them as well. Thus, the supernatural sanctions at their disposal are advertised and manipulated publicly; that is, the results of their supernatural machinations are public knowledge, though most of the processes by which they are activated are carried out in secret.

The Kafigelejo

Much of Kulebele supernatural power derives from the Kafigelejo which is represented by a small carved humanoid figure enveloped in country cloth and crowned with feathers.[60] The Kafigelejo is unique to Kulebele and is utilized by elder male and female Kulebele, although not all elder Kulebele are knowledgeable in dealing with it. The ability to make use of the Kafigelejo is dependent upon reaching the highest levels of esoteric Kulebele Poro knowledge and a willingness to dedicate one's resources, via sacrifices, to it in exchange for the powers of supernatural manipulation to be gained from it. The individual able to harness the power of the Kafigelejo derives power not only from the fetish itself, but also by the knowledge necessary to manipulate the powers of the fetish. Individuals possessing these powers are, indeed, fear-provoking. They should not be irritated, for non-Kulebele believe them to be quick to manifest their temper by invoking their supernatural abilities.

94

Kulebele who do not have direct access to the Kafigelejo have access through their elders who are in direct contact with it. Thus, all Kulebele have direct or indirect contact with their fetish. Those not in direct communication with the Kafigelejo must not see it. This interdiction includes non-Kulebele and Kulebele children, women of childbearing age, or any man or woman who has not fulfilled the ultimate Poro ascendency. As opposed to food sacrifices to lesser fetishes which may be consumed by women, children and non-initiates, the kola and meat sacrificed to the Kafigelejo may not be eaten by females, though any Kulebele male can eat them with impunity.[61]

With the Kafigelejo standing behind them, Kulebele are able to impose sanctions that conform to their standards of behavior vis-à-vis non-Kulebele. Further, elders have additional sanctions besides those of age, Poro standing and political prerogatives over lesser members of their own group, i.e., non-conforming Kulebele, can be and are threatened with Kafigelejo sanctions. However, elders who control Kafigelejo powers go to great lengths to avoid supernatural confrontations; they tolerate behavior from one another that would not be tolerated from non-Kulebele or young Kulebele. Thus, when the Nafoun Kulebele Poro wished to eliminate the superior Korhogo Kulebele Poro dancers from a funeral-dance competition in Nafoun, they enlisted the aid of a non-Kulebele possessing supernatural powers from a source other than the Kafigelejo. When the success of the supernatural attack was manifested by Korhogo's best dancers falling to the ground in convulsions during their dance, the Korhogo Kulebele *kafu* retaliated by imposing ritual shunning by his Poro group on all Nafoun rituals rather than by activating his Kafigelejo.[62]

Exogamous Marriage and Kafigelejo Sanctions

The backing of the Kafigelejo provides Kulebele with the opportunity to manifest behavior not allowed members of other groups. Most such behavior is aimed at keeping non-Kulebele at a distance in an effort to protect Kulebele exclusivity and to exploit and reinforce the privileges they carve out of the larger society for themselves. Kulebele ethnicity is strengthened by occupational secrets as well as marriage. As noted on pages 28-29,

Kulebele women do not ordinarily make exogamous marriages,[63] although over 31 per cent of the marriages involving Kulebele are exogamous. Kulebele women who seek to marry exogamously are discouraged by their lineage elders by threats of impending Kafigelejo sanctions, as are non-Kulebele men who seek them. A Kulebele female suspected of consorting with a non-Kulebele male is beaten. If her lover is caught, he, too, is beaten. Even if a female exogamous marriage is contracted with the approval of the woman's *narigba7a,* her husband is faced with forever placating his Kulebele in-laws with services and gifts of food. Demands are also made that he return to Kulebele all or most of the children borne to his wife. "To marry a Guleo woman isn't wise. If her kinsmen become angry with you, it is very dangerous, for there is a problem of sorcery."[64] Kulebele women, then, are not desirable as marriage partners because of the possibility of negative supernatural sanctions being applied by her kinsmen rather than because they are considered as "hardly human beings" as Himmelheber (1963:87) states.

Conversely, Kulebele men have little problem marrying exogamously. The same sanctions that are used to prevent women from marrying out are put into operation to bring women in. The Guleo male who seeks a non-Guleo bride can have recourse to Kafigelejo sanctions, and a non-Guleo who refuses his female dependent to a Guleo risks coping with negative supernatural sanctions. Few men or women are prepared to undertake the long and expensive procedure necessary to protect oneself from the Kafigelejo, particularly since there is no guarantee the process will be successful. The loss of a female by exogamous marriage is compensated by the return of at least one of her children to the lineage and by not having to undertake protective measures from the Kafigelejo. "If I don't give my daughter to Ngolo, the Kulebele will be very angry with me and that is very dangerous," complained a farmer.

As noted in Chapter 2, at least one child is sent to live with the mother's brother unless the child is an only child. The rest of the children are raised in their father's *kacolo.* Male children follow their father's profession and contribute financially to him. Thus the majority of children of Kulebele women who marry exogamously are lost to Kulebele in terms of labor and financial contributions. However, men who contract exogamous marriages sire children who will ultimately provide additional financial support or become the wives of Kulebele. The population, then, is able to expand more rapidly than if male endogamy were rigidly adhered to or female exogamy were allowed.

Thievery as an Economic Prerogative

The Kulebele exercise other economic prerogatives backed by supernatural sanctions vis-à-vis non-Kulebele. According to tradition, they were capable of changing themselves into hyenas in order to steal the livestock of non-Kulebele. Kulebele state that this measure was necessary only when a farmer refused to sell them an animal at a reasonable price. Non-Kulebele, however, maintain that price was rarely an issue. Rather, Kulebele simply stole whatever they pleased and their depredations were not confined to animals. Kulebele, in fact, have a bad reputation as thieves, though neither Kulebele nor Senufo nor Dyula farmers claim that sanctions are, or have ever been, taken against them. Kulebele feel confident of their position because of Kafigelejo backing and non-Kulebele fear to take measures against them for fear of supernatural retaliation.

As northern Ivory Coast became more densely populated and fields were expanded resulting in a decimation of the hyena population, the Kulebele "lost" their ability to turn into hyenas.[65] They began implementing their thievery by making themselves invisible. The reason for this change in technique, according to Kulebele, is that the elder and more knowledgeable Kulebele refused to pass their technique for changing into hyenas on to younger Kulebele. They feared the young men would become "stronger" than their elders. At about the same time the hyena population disappeared, the tourist art market was beginning to expand. Younger men began to realize an income disproportionate to that which they would have earned without the benefits of the new market. Young men were then beginning to have access to francs in amounts never before realized by any Kulebele and certainly more than their elders. A good portion of their income was handed over to their elders and the elders became directly dependent upon their *pibele* to provide needed and wanted francs. By withholding traditional Kulebele secrets, elders attempted to manipulate their *pibele* into producing for the tourist art market rather than depending in part on theft as a means of subsistence: the former was far more lucrative than the latter. Further, should

Kulebele become too zealous in their thievery in order to supplement what had been a meager living due to forced labor for the French, there was the possibility of victims appealing to French authorities against whom the Kafigelejo was not effective.[66]

The technique for becoming invisible can be purchased from non-Kulebele specialists for a rather high price. Depending upon the practitioner, the fee in 1974 could be as high as $250.[67] If a Guleo wishes to attain the ability of invisibility, it is necessary that he pay to learn the technique. He was not able to undertake this enterprise in the past since most of his income was turned over to his *kacolofolo* and he did not have access to large sums of money. Large expenditures were the prerogative of the *kacolofolo* who would be unwilling to invest so large a sum of money for a project that might ultimately be thwarted by French authorities. However, non-Kulebele believe that Kulebele still have the ability to become hyenas or to become invisible and still prey on farmers' livestock and belongings. They do not admit that such events occur less often than previously, though they make no attempts to stop Kulebele other than purchasing charms and "medicament" to prevent theft in general. There is no attempt to implement retributive action, either supernatural or by making reports to Ivorian authorities. Ivorian officials are, after all, Africans against whom Kafigelejo powers can be brought to play.[68] Thievery is, then, believed to be a Kulebele prerogative backed by the Kafigelejo.

Kulebele Rights to Trees

The appropriation of wood does not require nefarious practices such as changing oneself into a hyena or becoming invisible. Kulebele maintain control over the wood of trees whether useful for carving or not. Kulebele seeking wood for carving locate a suitable tree and approach the owner who may demand a nominal price for the tree. If Kulebele are not willing or able to pay the price, the tree is felled without payment. The owner dare not object for fear of Kafigelejo sanctions, but in any case few trees are considered so valuable that objections are raised when they are felled. Food-producing trees such as the baobab and the marcory, an oil-nut bearing tree, are considered unsuitable for carving as are imported fruit-bearing trees such as the orange, mango, papaya and cashew. If a supernatural entity is believed to inhabit the tree, which can often be determined by its peculiar configuration or location, the tree will not be cut down. Neither are trees in a *sinzang* felled.

Should a farmer need trees cleared off his land preparatory to planting a new field, it is obligatory that he enlist the aid of Kulebele, for only Kulebele can fell trees. As specialists in wood-handling techniques, they expect, and previously demanded, that they be consulted and employed for tree felling. Senufoland abounds in specialists and only a skilled individual in a particular art practices that art. Thus, there are specialists in mud-brick manufacture and house-building, thatch-tying, hunters, grave-diggers and griots, most of whom are *senambele* and none of whom constitutes a "caste." Specialists serve an apprenticeship under a master, which includes learning what Himmelheber (1963:100) has referred to as the "magical means." The population believes that specialties cannot be successfully practiced unless the proper magical formulas are known. The "magical means," however, are more often skill than magic. To fell a tree in a manner that it falls harmlessly in the proper place is not dependent upon magic but upon skill. Skilled Kulebele recognize this, though they also place importance on "luck" and the will of Kolocelo. Thus, when a 160-foot-tall, 25-foot-diameter bombax tree felled by a group of Kulebele fell across a road and onto a house, young Kulebele and non-Kulebele believed *ndebele*, Kolocelo and lack of proper magical intervention were responsible while the men who had worked on the felling blamed bad luck *(kapele)* and possibly the will of Kolocelo.

To fail to employ Kulebele to fell trees used to result in negative supernatural sanctions imposed by Kulebele. For their tree-felling services they were given a goat and provided with food while they were working as well as given first choice of the wood which may or may not have been suitable for carving. Wood unsuitable for carving would be used for cooking fires if there were Kulebele women available to cut it up. Wood not wanted by Kulebele would be given to those who had employed them.

While non-Kulebele are obliged to seek the services of Kulebele for tree-felling, Kulebele were also formerly obliged to perform this service. This symbiotic relationship is no longer viable in those areas where Kulebele are engaged in full-time carving for the tourist art market. Kulebele in the East are no longer willing to spend time felling a tree for a goat and a few meals when that time can be spent carving a mask or statue for francs. Thus Kulebele no longer insist on exercising their tree-felling rights and farmers are hard put to find Kulebele interested in cutting down trees unless they are useful for woodcarving. Only chiefs with national government ties can effectively recruit Kulebele for tree-felling for government purposes, e.g., the felling of a nuisance tree in front of the government bank or the felling of three large bombax trees where the government wants to sell lots.[69]

Sanctions Surrounding Work and Tools

Of particular importance are Kulebele sanctions surrounding their work and tools. All artisan groups living among the Senufo have similar sanctions against non-artisans seeing them at work or against handling their tools, e.g., *senambele* and Dyula are not allowed within Fonombele forge areas or allowed to touch the tools that are kept there. Neither may they handle the specialized knives that Fonombele women use for basket- and mat-making. These prohibitions do not apply to members of one's own group or to members of other *fijembele*. Thus, a Guleo may work the bellows for a Fonon who is making blades for him if another Fonon is not present to perform this task. *Senambele* and Dyula are traditionally forbidden to pick up or to handle Kulebele adzes and knives and the awls used by Kulebele women for mending calabashes. The sanctions purportedly imposed are those of the Kafigelejo which result in illness, madness or death unless the owner of the tools is pacified with gifts of food, cloth or cowries.

Kulebele perceive this interdiction as practical, for non-artisans do not know how to handle Kulebele knives, which are unique among knives and not held like other knives. The individual not familiar with them could easily cut himself. Thus, the taboo against non-artisans handling the knives prevents potentially unpleasant accidents. Further, the artisan's tools are the means by which he pursues his livelihood; they represent a capital investment. Non-artisans do not know how to handle these specialized tools in a manner that avoids damage to the tools. If a rock or the ground is struck with a blade, the blade is dulled and possibly nicked or damaged beyond repair, which would require that work be halted to resharpen the blade or even replace it. Should non-artisans have the opportunity to handle specialized tools, they may learn how to handle them efficiently and be able to practice the craft well enough to provide themselves with woodcarvings that would make inroads into the market traditionally Kulebele, which they want to prevent. Thus, by surrounding their tools with taboos, Kulebele prevent accidents to non-initiates, damage to tools, and, at the same time, protect their market.

Traditionally, Kulebele did not allow non-Kulebele to watch them carve. Kulebele were particularly stringent when rarely carved objects were being carved such as Poro and prestige items. Poro items are carved once a year when Poro activities commence at the beginning of the dry season in January. A carver does not consistently get as much practice carving objects such as helmet masks, face masks, large ritual drums, statues and trumpets as he does bowls, stools, mortars and pestles. Poro items used to be carved either in the privacy and quiet of the *sinzang* or in the carvers' quarters away from interruptions. Kulebele recognize that thought and concentration are necessary for successful execution, particularly of items they do not carve frequently or which are especially difficult.

One elder carver would tolerate and even solicit my presence when carving difficult helmet masks which he carved several times each month for the tourist market and with which he was familiar, but he had little patience with my presence when he undertook a helmet mask he had never carved before. With the former he worked swiftly and surely; with the latter he was unsure of himself, was given to long periods of speculation and planning and needed to consult with a carver more experienced than him with the type of mask he was carving. Privacy and lack of interruptions, then, are concomitants of success when unfamiliar items are being undertaken. Further, it is believed that if a non-carver observes a carver at work he will learn the "secrets" of the work, i.e., he will learn how tools are handled and the progress of the carving. With this knowledge he would be in a position to attempt carving himself, perhaps successfully.

To circumvent competition and insure privacy, Kulebele exploit several kinds of supernatural sanctions as well as physical threats. The Kafigelejo is ever present but other sanctions exist as well which generally arise from the future condition or content of the carving. For example, wood that is being carved to represent *ndebele* must not be seen in the making by non-Kulebele because the statue will ultimately be consumed by termites and the observer will then succumb to illness relative to the amount of damage done by termites. Thus, Kulebele work areas are avoided. Even someone who happened to pass by would be afflicted by illness if the carving of *ndebele* was accidentally observed. Non-initiates and women are forbidden to see some types of Poro masks danced or being transported to and from funeral sites.[70] The Poro further forbids them to see these masks, such as the *korobla*,[71] being carved. Carving in the *sinzang* thus functions in two ways: for the carver it insures relative privacy and for the Poro it insures that non-initates will not see certain genre of masks.

The physical sanction exercised by Kulebele is the right to sink their adzes into any non-artisan who observes them carving. The interloper is given the opportunity to placate the offended Guleo by offering food and livestock but should the carver not be satisfied with the offering, he may exercise his privilege of striking the intruder with his adze. Such a severe reaction to interference is reason enough to avoid Kulebele work areas. This sanction and sanctions of supernatural intervention provide the carvers with privacy and insure that his techniques will not be observed. However, Kulebele sanctions against observing them carve traditional objects are no longer extant in those areas where carvers are committed to the tourist art market. Kulebele in Korhogo will often go *en brousse* when they undertake a new or difficult item in order to get away from the traffic of other carvers, tourists and the demands of art traders. In the rural areas where farmers are respectful of Kafigelejo sanctions, carvers can work unharassed by interruptions from those they work with and for.

Finally, there are interdictions against non-artisans carving. Non-artisans do carve in areas where Kulebele are not found, and at one time Kulebele were few enough in number that their interdiction could not be enforced. However, as Kulebele populations increased and carvers began migrating in order to find work, it was necessary that non-artisan carvers competing for the same market as Kulebele be discouraged from the competition. This was done through the auspices of the Kafigelejo. Non-artisans were forbidden to carve not only Poro items, but household and prestige objects as well.

An example of what non-artisans who are carving can expect at the hands of Kulebele was manifested in 1974 in Touvre. A young Guleo from Kouto decided to migrate to Touvre. It is close enough to Kouto that he could visit kinsmen yet far enough away that he could be independent. There are abundant wood sources nearby, the village is large enough that carving commissions would be forthcoming for several years and there is abundant and relatively good farmland adjacent to the village. However, when he arrived in Touvre, he found that the villagers had no need for a carver for two farmers were providing the villagers with the wood items they needed. The young Guleo reported the situation to the Kouto Kulebele *kafu* who walked the 15 kilometers to Touvre where he accosted the Touvre *kafu* and elders. He "yelled and yelled" while threatening the village with Kafigelejo sanctions so effectively that the farmer-carvers gave up carving and the young carver immigrated to the village where he has resided without competition; thus, his market is assured. Indeed, the village has proved to be so lucrative in terms of commissions that two more Kulebele have immigrated to it.

The interdictions on all the above behaviors concerned with carving, with the exception of handling tools, have been lifted in the areas where Kulebele are committed to the tourist art market. Korhogo Kulebele have accepted several non-Kulebele as apprentices. Not only do non-Kulebele have more freedom to move about Kulebele work areas but they are being incorporated into the ritual and economic spheres of Kulebele life. Non-Kulebele apprentices are required to join Kulebele Poro and contribute labor and money to their *jatugu*. Whether or not they contract marriages with Kulebele women remains to be seen. Two of the *nubombele* are old unmarried Fonombele and the remainder are *senambele* too young to marry as yet.

Kulebele still retain an unsavory reputation as a result of their past activities. Farmers still claim that Kulebele are the "most evil" of all people living in Senufoland: they are quick to anger and to kill people supernaturally and they persist in their thievery. Kulebele, on the other hand, maintain that they are far "nicer" to farmers than in the past. Indeed, they teach farmers how to carve while, at the same time, insisting it is not really acceptable that farmers carve, and they are not as quick to kill or steal as before. As one Kulebele stated: "We don't need the farmers anymore. We can carve for the whites. Why should we do anything to the farmers anymore?"

In the past Kulebele employed supernatural sanctions designed to protect their ethnicity and exclusive rights over carving. By surrounding their activities with an aura of supernatural sanctions Kulebele strove to protect the specialized knowledge used in woodcarving and to maintain their exclusive hold on the carving market.

As Kulebele become inundated with orders for the tourist art market, their need to protect a limited traditional market has become less urgent. The demands of the tourist market insures sufficient work for all Kulebele who wish to carve. Indeed, there is such an abundance of work that non-Kulebele can be absorbed without threatening the income of Kulebele. In view of the plethora of work, Kulebele no longer employ negative supernatural sanctions against the cutting of trees by non-Kulebele. Their interest lies with carving for the tourist market rather than felling trees for non-Kulebele. Further, those who are engaged in carving for the tourist market no longer prohibit non-Kulebele from seeing them carve either tourist or traditional items. Only Kulebele who are still dependent upon traditional commissions surround their work with negative sanctions.

Kulebele have responded to an expanded market in a manner similar to Zulu blacksmiths in the face of Shaka's demand for innumerable new weapons. The expanded market resulted in the "hocus-pocus and secrecy" being eliminated and blacksmithing "turned into an open and flourishing industry" (Ritter 1973:81).

7

Exploitation of
New Economic Opportunities

Wealth is an ideal aspired to by all Kulebele. A young man who is a hard worker is expected to become wealthy. If he does not, it is because he has had bad luck *(kapele)* or has not handled his assets wisely. While Kolocelo bestows good luck *(kacana)* and bad luck indiscriminately, one may have the misfortune of having received bad luck. This, however, can be rectified to some degree by hard work and careful husbanding of resources and investments.

A healthy male between the ages of 12 and 45 who does not work consistently is considered irresponsible and does not enjoy the status deserving of his particular age group. The non-worker provokes the contempt and suspicions of other Kulebele. A young man who is not diligent in his work is subjected to a hierarchy of progressively severe social sanctions. Initially, scolding and criticism by the young man's *kacolofolo* are employed. If this is not effective, the *kafu* and larger kin group become involved in criticizing which eventually evolves into public haranguing and shunning by peers and older kinsmen. If he still does not conform, food may be withheld and he may be denied sleeping facilities. Further, since he is shunned by other Kulebele, he is forced to associate with non-Kulebele companions. Associations with non-Kulebele result in an even more tenuous relationship with the Kulebele community for all out-groups are believed to engage in a variety of undesirable behaviors. Thus, the man who does not work has problems which become compounded, for not only does he not work but he keeps company with strangers.

Unless the recalcitrant young man mends his ways, he becomes a peripheral member of Kulebele society. He must seek his own lodgings which, in Korhogo requires renting quarters and making arrangements for meals, both of which require money which, in turn, requires working. In rural areas, the non-worker does not have the opportunities for escaping the criticism of kinsmen since rental units do not exist and farmers in villages will not provide quarters for fear of ensuing conflicts resulting from providing a haven for a non-conforming Guleo. Further, the non-worker will not be given a wife by any Kulebele man and usually is unable to find a non-Kulebele who would be willing to give him a wife. Sons-in-law are potential sources of income and no man is willing to invest a daughter or female dependent in a non-productive husband.

Traditional Wealth Accumulation and Investment

Work and maximizing earnings by investing in wealth-producing ventures is traditional with Kulebele. They have exploited all the economic possibilities open to them: carving, farming and investing and trading in livestock. Activities such as iron-working, brasscasting and weaving were not open to Kulebele just as the business of carving wood was not open to non-Kulebele. Other ethnic groups maintained control of particular trade items, e.g., Dyula were cloth merchants, Fulani controlled milk products and Tagwana monopolized the kola-nut trade. Kulebele exchanged carved wood objects for cowries and carvers living in host-villages received food, livestock and housing as well.

Kulebele farming was for subsistence needs, though the small surpluses that might occur were traded at local markets for cowries. Small livestock such as chickens, guinea fowl, goats and sheep were purchased with cowries and also received from *jatugu*. Small stock was retained for eventual consumption, sacrifices or sale. Cattle were purchased for funeral rites and not generally sold, though their offspring were sometimes sold. The buying and selling of horses involved traveling by foot to what is now Mali, purchasing the animals and walking them to northern Ivory Coast where they were sold. Ordinarily, Kulebele bought one horse at a time in Mali to herd to and sell in Ivory Coast.

The goods sold and traded by Kulebele were confined to items they produced themselves such as carvings, farm products and livestock. Some individuals were involved in all three means of earning a livelihood and maximizing wealth while others, the finest carvers, were engaged in carving only. The proceeds from the latter's efforts were invested in livestock or hoarded and managed by the *narigba7afolo* or eldest uterine brother. Other men devoted most of their energies to farming but their excess income was also invested in livestock. The means of accumulating wealth were diversified sufficiently so that should one avenue fail, there were others to fall back on.

As various members of a kin group were engaged in diverse income-producing activities, a means of subsistence was virtually guaranteed all Kulebele. Indeed, a *kacolofolo* would often direct the activities of his *pibele* so as to diversify their efforts which insured that all wealth-producing activities were pursued. Thus, women were occupied with farming as were the young people, all of whom were under the supervision of the *kacolofolo*. Teenage boys who were not occupied with farming cared for livestock, and adult men were engaged in either farming or carving and, occasionally, long-distance trading of horses.

Accumulated capital was ultimately hoarded or invested in cattle. Hoarded cowries provided a ready source of general-purpose money for day-to-day expenses as well as for ritual expenses such as Poro fees and funeral cloths. Cowries were also distributed at funerals to relatives of the deceased and to funeral performers such as Poro dancers and non-Poro singers and dancers. Cowries were used to pay specialists for their services, e.g., thatchers for thatching roofs, Fonombele for making knives and adzes, and grave-diggers. Food, cloth and livestock as well as services could be bought with cowries. Cowries, however, are not self-multiplying; they do not multiply except by one's adding to them from cowries earned from income-producing activities such as carving or selling foodstuffs or livestock. Livestock, on the other hand, reproduces itself. Thus, Kulebele invested cowries in chickens, guinea fowls, goats, sheep and cattle, and, occasionally, horses, all of which could be sold if the need arose for cowries.

Cattle and horses are major investments for they require a large outlay of cowries.[72] Further, cattle fall prey to diseases. Indeed, whole herds have been decimated within a few weeks. Herds are kept in crowded corrals at night which, during the rainy season, are several inches deep in mud. Crowding and constant dampness result in the rapid spread of disease. Fulani are employed by Kulebele to look after their cattle. In exchange for their services, they received cowries in the past, and receive francs today, and are given milking rights. They consistently over-milk nursing cows and calves die from lack of milk which further enhances the risk of investing in cattle.[73] A final risk is theft by nomadic Fulani who, according to Kulebele, are assisted by the Fulani whom they hire to care for their cattle. The problems surrounding investment of capital in cattle are reasons why Kulebele have turned to other investment opportunities that have arisen as a result of contact with the West.

Antique Art Market Trading

The arrival of the French in Ivory Coast resulted in a means of income not previously existent, namely, the market for antique woodcarvings. The wealth of the most affluent Kulebele today is based on monies earned by dealing in "old wood." Rumor among non-Kulebele suggests that Kulebele acquired old carvings by stealing them or encouraging others to steal them and Kulebele are secretive about the methods they employed in collecting old carvings. Kulebele are not opposed to handling and trading stolen carvings. As one master carver commented: "If someone steals everything out of the *sinzang,* it is okay [with me] because the farmers would have to commission new carvings and I'm looking for money."[74]

Stolen carvings still find their way to the Kulebele, brought by traders for repair or reworking. Four large sacred Poro trumpets *(numa7a)* brought to Kulebele to be carved in bas-relief were known to have been stolen.[75] An attempt was made to keep them out of sight while they were being carved in case a farmer might pass by and see them. Trumpets would be found in the Kulebele work area only if they were stolen, for Kulebele do not use them or keep them for ritual purposes. Thus, if Kulebele were seen with trumpets, it would be known that they were stolen and restitution, if demanded, would have to be made in the form of francs, cowries and livestock.

Kulebele were ideally situated as middlemen between the French who sought antique carvings and those who owned them, for they provided new carvings for the *sinzang* and thus knew when pieces were being replaced. As members of farmers' Poro, they had access to *sinzang* other than their own. They readily knew what old pieces were or would be available. On the other hand, they were recognized by the French as connoisseurs of carvings. In this capacity they were called upon to identify carvings and, after tourist market production was in full swing, to authenticate them too. Indeed, Kulebele are able to identify by its style which group, whether Kulebele or Fonombele, carved any given piece. The style is also a clue to relative age. The condition of the wood and patination are also clues to authenticity and Kulebele are able to determine whether or not a patina is artificial or the result of use.

Kulebele have been involved in dealing with the sale of old carvings since at least the 1940's. As more and more items were stolen, Poro installed watchmen in their *sinzang* to protect their ritual paraphernalia, making theft more difficult. Kulebele and traders turned to other means of obtaining old carvings, which they continue to practice: the exchange of new carvings for old. Exchanges of this sort, when involving traders, are instigated by the trader. He commissions traditional new carvings and then attempts to exchange them for old ones in the rural areas.

Kulebele sometimes obtain old carvings when a Poro commissions a new carving. The carver commissioned to make the new carving offers to accept the piece it is to replace as payment for his work rather than being paid in francs. The old carving is then sold to foreign dealers for a higher price than the carver would have received if the Poro had paid francs for his work.[76] Kulebele are recognized by farmers as being experts in affairs concerning carving and carvings, whereas farmers are considered to have no knowledge of the business of trading or selling carvings. They prefer to do business with the traditional experts, the Kulebele, rather than with foreign and strange traders whom they regard with suspicion. Traders do not have the time to cultivate the confidence of farmers, a process which may require months of visits and possibly ends unfruitfully. Thus, the Kulebele position as traditional experts of carving made it possible for them to exploit a new and lucrative market, namely that of dealing in antique woodcarvings.

Tourist Art Trading

As noted above, Kulebele were carving for the French by the early 20th century. When forced labor ended not long before the middle of the century, the tourist art market became a small but rewarding means of earning francs. As the market expanded, younger Kulebele began migrating to Korhogo to take advantage of its potential. This trend has continued until eastern rural areas are almost decimated of all but elder men and their female dependents. Carving for the tourist art market and for francs has been subsumed into an already extant practice of carving for cowries, livestock and foodstuffs.

The demands of the tourist market have grown to the point where everything produced by Kulebele is saleable and all Kulebele who wish to participate are easily absorbed. Carving for the tourist market provides a larger and steadier income than either carving for the traditional market or farming and is a means of accumulating the wealth upon which new fortunes are being based. Profits from carving are used to buy a motorbike, residential lot, build a house, and carvings to sell in the tourist art market.

Dealing in tourist carvings was a natural outgrowth from carving for French administrators. As more commissions were received for carvings, those who received them and did not have time to fulfill them commissioned their kinsmen to execute the carvings. Customarily, chiefs were the point of contact for French administrators. In Korhogo the chief of the Korhogo Kulebele became the disseminator of commissions for the French and was dealing in new carvings by the end of the 1940's. The prerogatives of dealing in carvings were initially held by the Korhogo Kulebele chief's *narigba7a*. As the market expanded, Kulebele who had the capital to invest in speculative buying became involved. The tourist market is still monopolized by the original investors, but younger men are beginning to become involved as they accumulate capital from carving for the tourist market and begin to speculate in carvings done by men who mass-produce them.

As more time was spent overseeing the mass-production of carvings and more income was realized from tourist dealing, less time was spent on carving by men who became dealers. Income was ultimately invested in an inventory of carvings commissioned on a speculative basis, in anticipation of sales rather than waiting for commissions. Kulebele dealers became middlemen who anticipated future sales, and their dwellings have become places where a wide variety of carvings can be viewed and considered by prospective buyers. Kulebele middlemen bulk-buy mass-produced carvings *en brousse*. The carvings they buy have not been painted, stained, or waxed, which are techniques of finishing applied to tourist art market items. The dealer arranges for the transport of the carvings to Korhogo where they are finished by his *pibele* before being offered for sale. A dealer's *pibele* include his own sons, if he has any, and a variety of other male dependents.

For example, one successful Guleo dealer's *pibele* include two of his own sons in their early teens and three teenage sons of one of his wives' sisters who are not Kulebele and who have been sent to Korhogo to learn to carve or to attend school. One of the wives' sister's sons is occupied only with carving. He produces for the tourist market, the proceeds of which he keeps. The finishing work and other labor he does for the dealer is in return for a place to sleep and meals provided by the dealer. The other two wives' sisters' sons attend lycée and do not carve. They finish tourist market carvings in return for room and board. The dealer's two sons also attend school but they do some carving for the tourist market for pocket money. As the dealer's sons, they are expected to perform whatever chores their father requests. None of these teenagers receives money for the work he does for the dealer. If a dealer's *pibele* are too young to finish carvings or are female, he must pay boys to finish carvings for him. Labor, however, is cheap and a boy may receive only 100 CFA (50¢) for several days' work.

Because of their exclusive position as middlemen, Kulebele dealers were able to control prices paid to carvers producing for the tourist market. When foreign dealers, such as Hausa and Senegalese, began arriving in Korhogo, the only means they had of breaking into the market was to offer prices higher than those of the Kulebele traders. When carvers began selling directly to Hausa and Senegalese, Kulebele dealers attempted to protect their exclusivity as middlemen and there were several confrontations between them and the foreign dealers. Kulebele threatened to invoke supernatural sanctions, but there are no reports of mysterious or supernaturally induced disasters befalling any of the foreign traders. The Senegalese and Hausa rapidly gained recognition as paying better prices than Kulebele traders and, rather than taking advantage of kinship ties to defer payment as do many Kulebele traders, they pay immediately and in full.

Not all Kulebele dealers use kinship as a means of manipulating payment to their advantage. The practice is limited to one important Kulebele *kafu* and his maternal and paternal kinsmen, who are recognized by other Kulebele as being greedy and are surreptitiously criticized for it. They insist on lower prices, using the reason that as Kulebele they are entitled to a discount when buying from Kulebele. Further, they rarely pay in full even after a favorable price has been agreed on, which is a sharp business practice when used inter-ethnically but one considered highly irregular intra-ethnically. Because these dealers "cut men's throats," they are forced to deal with rural carvers who have little contact with foreign dealers and who are generally the less able carvers. These Kulebele middlemen are also sold carvings which have been rejected by foreign dealers because of poor workmanship or design.

Kulebele traders sell their merchandise to out-of-town African and European dealers. Dealers who are not based in Korhogo have little opportunity to see the better quality work currently being done since most of it is by commission only and ultimately destined for discriminating collectors. Further, they are not willing to pay the higher prices for the better work. Indeed, because they are not knowledgeable about prices in Korhogo, they usually are charged high prices for poor work. They are generally interested in the bulk-buying of tourist market items as the lowest-possible price for resale to tourists in cities such as Dakar, Cotonou, Douala and Abidjan. It is with dealers of this ilk that Kulebele traders do business and rarely with dealers buying for the discriminating African art market in the West.

A new marketing opportunity has recently developed that is exploited by Kulebele. The Office National de l'Artisanat d'Art de Côte d'Ivoire was created by the Ivorian government as a means of encouraging the continuation of indigenous arts and as a part of a scheme to attract tourists. The projected plan is to establish ateliers throughout Ivory Coast where craftsmen can be seen working and where the government will sell arts and crafts. The government hopes to eliminate Senegalese and Hausa art dealers, to become the major source of Ivorian arts and crafts and to grant exclusive rights to wholesalers overseas. According to a catalogue printed by the Office National de l'Artisanat d'Art de Côte d'Ivoire and the Ministère d'Etat Chargé du Tourism (c1973), the ONAA guarantees the origin of its inventory, i.e., Senufo-style carvings originate in Senufoland, Dyula-patterned weavings are woven by Dyula, etc.[77] With this purpose in mind, Kulebele dealers have been contacted and four letters of appointment as official government dealers have been awarded. The Kulebele who were awarded the letters now conceive of the government as their most lucrative customer and expect to charge retail prices. However, they do not expect to pay higher prices to the carvers. Thus, they pay from 1500 to 2500 CFA for a large drum for which they will ask 10,000 CFA from the government.[78] It will be recalled that the best carvers do not deal with Kulebele traders because of the poor prices they pay. The better carvers deal with Hausa and Senegalese traders, who are expressly those the ONAA is trying to put out of business.

Improved Real Estate Investment

In the mid-1960's the Ivorian government ordered that Korhogo be razed in order to impose a standardized city plan which included building concrete-block houses according to predetermined designs. By the late 1960's, all elder Kulebele engaged in the tourist art market had constructed concrete-block houses in which their families were settled. Indeed, the Kulebele take pride in the fact that they were among the first in Quartier Koko to construct concrete-block houses. Even before the government imposed building regulations, Kulebele had begun building mud-brick houses with concrete exterior plaster and corrugated-metal roofs. They were amenable to the new housing codes and financially able to concur with them.

Until the 1960's, the townspeople of Korhogo provided immigrants with dwelling places and provided them with food until they were settled, which accorded with traditional practices. The residents of Korhogo did not solicit payment for the use of empty huts or sleeping places. Huts were cheaply built and most concessions had at least one room set aside for visitors. The government program of the 1960's made it necessary to build expensive concrete-block houses. *Kacolofolobele* were not willing or able to build guest houses of expensive construction though, in keeping with the ideals of hospitality, an attempt was made to maintain an extra room for visitors. However, the number of emigrants that could be accommodated into a rigidly structured and gridded town was less than could be accommodated in an organically expanding one.

As Korhogo began offering more and more benefits, such as a major everyday market, government services, medical facilities and schools, people were attracted from far away and the town increased in population until kinship and friendship networks could no longer absorb the large number of immigrants. Those residents with capital to invest began buying residental lots and building houses to rent. Primary among those who invested in rental property were Kulebele who had large hoards of cowries and francs earned from their antique and tourist art market activities.

Kulebele had more capital than they had ever had and needed new investment opportunities. Cattle had lost favor as a means of capital investment because of the problems inherent in keeping herds as noted above. Indeed, one Kulebele *kafu* lost 15 head of cattle to disease within two weeks, which represents a potential sum of 300,000 CFA which is approximately $1,500. Improved real estate was not monopolized by specialists and provided an investment that realized monthly returns in the form of rent. Further, there was no risk of the holdings being lost or succumbing to disease as had happened with their cattle. As the benefits of investing in improved real estate became apparent, wealthy Kulebele sold their cattle to invest in lots upon which they built rental units. They continued to maintain some cattle, however, in order to meet contributions for funerals, but the bulk of their wealth was now invested in an inventory of carvings and real estate.

Alternatives To Real Estate Investment and Tourist Art Dealings

The opportunity to invest in improved real estate does not exist in the rural area. With the exception of Kolia, no Kulebele villages have been subjected to development programs. Kolia was not made a *sous-préfecture* until 1974, at which time the new *sous-préfet* decreed that the residents would have a year to conform to the modern building codes. The response of Kolia Kulebele has been to buy lots and to begin buying cement for building-blocks as they are able to afford it. Currently, there is no pattern of emigration to Kolia and no pressure on extant housing. Thus, the opportunity to rent space does not exist.

Kulebele in Kolia are not deeply involved in the tourist art market but are more committed to farming. There is no pressure on the land so that land for cash-cropping as well as for subsistence farming is readily available. Kulebele in Kolia not only farm for subsistence but are also occupied with growing cotton which the government buys. Kolia Kulebele and other western

114

Kulebele are also still involved with carving household items for the traditional market such as food stirrers, mortars and pestles, bowls and stools with which eastern Kulebele rarely concern themselves any longer because of the low prices they bring. Western Kulebele still invest extra income in cattle which are cared for by Fulani and are subject to the high risk of loss and disease.

Kolia Kulebele who wish to enhance their fortunes do so by migrating to urban areas for a variety of reasons. For example, four full-brothers migrated to Abidjan where they engaged in dealing in motorbikes and cloth. Another man has moved to a village near Boundiali to carve for the *sous-préfet* of Boundiali, and his two half-brothers and their families have migrated to Korhogo to carve for the tourist market. The latter two men have attracted secondary school students who are kinsmen of varying degrees, for there is no secondary school in Kolia.

Kolia Kulebele are educating their young people whereas Korhogo Kulebele still keep some boys out of school to help with the business of preparing mass-purchased carvings for the tourist market. Education of the young is considered with far more seriousness in Kolia than in Korhogo. It is through education that the Kolia Kulebele hope their youth will find jobs that pay well and will help them realize their aspirations to wealth. In Korhogo, education is not the only means of attaining wealth for Kulebele. Older, illiterate men have attained considerable wealth through their antique and tourist art dealings and real estate. Indeed, some of the most dismal students are the sons and dependents of wealthy Kulebele. For example, it has taken seven years for one young man to finish three years of lycée, and three other dependents of wealthy men failed to pass any of their classes during the two-and-one-half years I had contact with them. They were passed to higher grades only because their wealthy kinsmen gave money gifts to the appropriate school authorities.

Kulebele have traditionally sought out opportunities to maximize their earnings by investing capital in wealth-producing ventures. Formerly, their capital was hoarded and invested in livestock. As larger fortunes were realized through antique dealing and tourist carving, Kulebele invested in stocks of mass-produced carvings.

Government-imposed housing regulations resulted in a shortage of housing space in Korhogo. Kulebele were among those who took advantage of the opportunity to build rental units from which earnings rapidly accumulated. Rents and proceeds from tourist art dealings were and are invested in larger stocks of tourist carvings and more improved real estate. Profits are no longer invested in cattle by Korhogo Kulebele because of the high risk involved and because higher profit-yielding opportunities are available.

Rural Kulebele do not have the opportunity to invest in rental properties because there is no demand for rentals *en brousse*. They still invest in cattle and in Kolia, the education of children is expected to result in future earning potential.

Summary and Conclusion

In the preceding chapters I have described the responses of a group of woodcarvers in Northern Ivory Coast to the economic opportunities of the tourist art market, to contact with Islam and to state policies aimed at modernization. Many social changes have occurred, but they are not all of the same order; some are elaborations of traditional Kulebele themes, some parallel traditional *senambele* themes not possible for Kulebele in the past and some are shared by others in Senufoland but have no precedence in the past. All of these changes, however, are interconnected and not necessarily discrete.

Elaborations on Traditional Kulebele Themes

Kulebele have always migrated and they continue to do so, but the rationale behind their motives to migrate were very different in the past when they sought villages where there would be a demand for their products. They were dependent upon host-villagers to buy their wares, and villagers provided housing, food and land use-rights for immigrant carvers. The relationship was symbiotic even though fraught with anxiety on the part of the host-villagers who feared Kulebele supernatural powers. Kulebele did not congregate in large numbers in any host-village but spaced themselves throughout Senufoland in order not to compete with one another. Thus, the small extended family of carvers in any one village could be provided for by villagers without creating a stress on their resources.

Kulebele continue to migrate today in connection with their work but the goals that underlie their motives bear little resemblance to traditional migration. Kulebele involved in the tourist art market choose host-villages on the basis of neighboring wood resources and accessibility to Korhogo where tourist art market dealers operate. These carvers are not concerned with the needs of host-villagers and do not look to them to buy Kulebele carvings. The market for Kulebele wares is alien to host-villages' needs and Kulebele are now resident strangers with few social and economic ties to their hosts. Host-villagers still provide housing and land-use rights for Kulebele but they are not able or willing to provide food for the increasing numbers of Kulebele who settle amongst them to exploit free housing, abundant wood resources and to obtain land use-rights for subsistence and cash crops.

Another traditional Kulebele value that has been elaborated is the accumulation of wealth. Kulebele speak of wealthy ancestors with pride when describing the size of their herds, the number of their wives and dependents and the number of cowries that overflowed the large baskets they secreted in their huts. However, none of these ancestors was able to accumulate the wealth that Kulebele now realize. The basis for wealth-accumulation today is carving for the tourist art market; the resulting profits allow carvers to become dealers in tourist and antique carvings and to invest in improved real estate, which generates additional capital for further investment.

Improved property as an investment is the result of government town-planning and building restrictions and is not monopolized by any particular ethnic group as were many of the economic possibilities in the traditional context, such as craft occupations, certain kinds of trade, such as the cloth or kola-nut trade, or the care of cattle or marketing of milk. The opportunity to become a landlord is determined by access to capital, not ethnic affiliation, and Kulebele, because of tourist art market earnings, have the capital to exploit the new economic opportunity that resulted from the razing of Korhogo and new building codes. Today they are less frequently dependent upon Fulani to care for their cattle because capital is seldom invested in cattle.

Thus, while migration and the accumulation of wealth are traditional expectations and goals, the context of migration and the form of wealth-accumulation have changed, both of which have resulted in greater independence of Kulebele from reciprocal relationships with other local ethnic groups. Kulebele now exploit their rights as strangers in host-villages while generally ignoring their obligations to provide carvings and to cut down trees.

Echoes of Traditional Senambele Themes

As long as Kulebele have been in Senufoland, which is probably no more than 200 years, they have been witness to Senufo expansionistic political maneuvers and wars. By the mid-19th century the Kingdom of Kenedougou had been established,[79] which included most of the traditional Kulebele villages. The establishment of Kenedougou did not result in peace and stability; subject villages under chiefs hostile to the kings of Kenedougou were a constant source of concern as they tried to establish their autonomy and assert their political power.

Ultimately, Kenedougou disintegrated at the end of the 19th century as a result of conflicts with Samori and the French. The area embraced by the kingdom and the areas to the West and South that had been conquered by Samori, who was captured by the French in 1898, fragmented into numerous small states headed by Senufo chiefs whose wealth and power were measured, in part, by the number of subjects at their command. The Poro of important chiefs were large and provided them with a well-disciplined military resource.

The small groups of Kulebele scattered among the various *senambele* chiefdoms did not follow the pattern of expansionism, conflict and political manipulations practiced by powerful *senambele* chiefs. Although some Kulebele achieved considerable wealth relative to many *senambele*, their numbers were few and disbursed and no Kulebele chief had the opportunity to accumulate enough *pibele* to become an important political presence. Today, however, Kulebele engaged in the tourist art market are able to congregate in large numbers and even those who migrate to rural villages are able to stay in close contact with their *narigba7a* and their chiefs; with tourist art market earnings they are able to purchase motorbikes and transport their families by public transportation, all of which permits a mobility not possible in the past.

The nexus of the tourist art market for Kulebele is Korhogo and they no longer need to space themselves throughout Senufo-land in search of work. Thus, their numbers are far more concentrated today and their chiefs are in closer contact and conflict than in the past as they attempt to extend their suzerainty over carvers who immigrate to Korhogo. Rural Kulebele chiefs attempt to maintain control over emigrant carvers from their villages while urban Kulebele chiefs seek to assume command over immigrant rural Kulebele. Indeed, in Korhogo, two Kulebele chiefs struggle over the allegiance of immigrant Kulebele and accept non-Kulebele as apprentices who are obliged to join their Kulebele sponsor's Poro. Kulebele chiefs who are in conflict with each other and attempt to extend their suzerainty over ever-increasing numbers of carvers and to increase the numbers of men initiated in their Poro are following a *senambele* model with which they have long been acquainted but were not able to realize in the past.

Other behavior patterns indigenous to *senambele* have been emulated by Kulebele. Traditionally, most *senambele* men did not marry until they were in their thirties or older[80] and genealogies of elder Kulebele men indicate that they were often in their forties before they married the first time. However, men who were members of *senambele* chiefly lineages married at an earlier age than the rest of the population (Person 1973a:216) and some *senambele* chiefs were married in their teens and twenties.[81]

Because they are able to amass wealth at an earlier age than in the past and because of their future economic potential in the tourist art market and as landlords, Kulebele now marry at an earlier age, a tendency also true of urban *senambele* and Fonombele.[82] Kulebele chiefs encourage earlier marriage for Kulebele men and arrange for first marriages for favored male dependents while they are still in their early 20's. Many Kulebele men now have three wives by the time they are in their mid-30's and several children. Early marriage implies wealth and the multiple wives and many children of a chief's male *pibele* are counted among a chief's dependents, which adds to his status.

Kulebele are traditionally matrilineal, but there is evidence in their kinship terminology of incipient patrilineality. In the case of the present Korhogo Kulebele *kafu*, his secular political role will be passed on matrilineally but his religico-Poro role will be inherited by one of his sons as a result of the conversion of his sisters' sons to Islam. While both of these changes are a result of Islamic contact, Kulebele responses parallel those of important *senambele* lineages that control considerable wealth, land and people. Politically powerful *senambele* lineages reckon kinship matrilineally and Ego is a member of his/her mother's *narigba7a,* but political authority and position are inherited patrilineally as a result of contact with powerful Dyula leaders who are Muslims and patrilineal. Increased personal wealth and economic opportunity may weaken matrilineal organization,[83] but in the case of Kulebele the previously extant *senambele* model provided the pattern adopted by them.

While conversion to Islam has thus far been minimal among Kulebele, several of the converts are members of the chiefly Korhogo Kulebele *narigba7a.* The reasons for their conversion are not clear, but many important *senambele* chiefs are Muslim converts, including those of the principle *senambele* lineage in Korhogo, several of whom are also important political personages in the Ivorian government. It is through these individuals that the Korhogo Kulebele *kafu* and his *pibele* have contact with opportunities offered by the government to carve in government *atéliers* and have received letters of authorization to act as government suppliers of Kulebele carvings.

The majority of *senambele* is matrilineal and not Muslims and in the past men did not marry until they were in their 30's. Patrilineal succession of political rights, conversion to Islam, early marriage of men, and Poro with enough initiates to create the impession of political and military strength occur only in chiefly lineages. Changes in Kulebele social organization that parallel those of *senambele* are based upon a chieflyl *senambele* model as Kulebele strive to emulate politically important *senambele* lineages.

Innovative Responses and Unfamiliar Patterns

Some of the changes that have occurred in Kulebele social organization are not based upon traditional Kulebele or *senambele* themes. These include earlier autonomy of adult males, dilution of the political powers of Kulebele chiefs, male/female conflict, the loss of some supernatural behaviors and sanctions, the revelation of carving techniques to *senambele* and the alienation of Kulebele from their *senambele* hosts.

121

Autonomy of young Kulebele men is the result of tourist art market participation, earlier marriage and government policies concerned with modernization. Because of government regulations that limit the number and kinds of buildings that can be constructed on a residential lot, the heads of households, *kacolofobele,* are not able to provide housing for all of their male dependents who marry and begin families at a younger age than in the past. As noted above, men still in their 20's are able to begin acquiring wives. Because of their tourist art market earnings, they are now able to buy a lot, build a house and establish their own *kacolo* at an age when, in the past, they would still have been dependent upon and obligated to a *kacolofo.*

Because men need to save their earnings in order to establish their own *kacolo,* they resist contributing the major part of their income to their *kacolofolo.* A large portion of their earnings is saved towards the purchase of a lot or the construction of a house. Once the new family is established in its own *kacolo,* which is removed from those of other Kulebele because of the centrifugal expansion pattern of Korhogo, the new *kacolofolo* contributes even less to his elders because he needs his earnings to support his household.

Today, elders have little control over the economic resources of their dependents and the rift is even more severe after dependents establish independent *kacolobele.* Thus, though many Kulebele are now permanently settled in Korhogo, they are scattered throughout the northwestern quarter of the town and it is therefore virtually impossible for the two aged Kulebele chiefs in Korhogo to keep track of their activities or extract financial contributions from them. The irony of the situation is that Kulebele chiefs aid and abet earlier marriage for their male dependents in accordance with ideals extrapolated from chiefly *senambele* lineages and in hopes of enhancing their own status, but by doing so, they weaken their political and economic controls as young men establish their new families in autonomous *kacolobele.*

The economic stresses experienced by *kacolofobele* are greater in Korhogo than in rural settings. Lots and houses are expensive to buy and build, though once the investment has been made, maintenance and utility expenses are virtually non-existent. In 1975, only six Kulebele houses had electricity. These houses were occupied by Kulebele; electricity was not installed in any rental units. Further, men are traditionally responsible for clothing their families, paying medical expenses, which include traditional medical treatment for supernaturally induced health problems, and meat for the family diet. Korhogo Kulebele men must also pay for food staples, such as corn and rice, because of the shortage of farmland around Korhogo. Indeed, Kulebele women contribute little to the economy of the *kacolo,* and men must occasionally even provide the money for such items as soap, thread used in plaiting their wives' hair, pot-scrubbers and for having corn milled into flour.

The idleness of Kulebele women and the added economic responsibilities placed upon men have resulted in friction between men and women that is not apparent in the rural context. Men migrate to Korhogo in order to participate in the tourist art market, but once they are settled there they are locked into an ever-increasing spiral of demands upon their resources as their families increase in size and since their wives contribute little to the household economy. However, by maintaining a rural-type diet, which contains little meat or rice and consists of vegetable sauces and *to7,* a corn-flour and water mush,[84] and by purchasing clothing for their wives only after many days, or even weeks, of importunity, carvers are able to save money for capital investments.

Other new patterns of behavior concern Kulebele relationships with *senambele.* The alienation of migrant Kulebele from their *senambele* hosts has been discussed above, but there have also been other changes in *senambele*/Kulebele relationships. Kulebele committed to the tourist art market no longer impose all of the supernatural sanctions at their disposal in their relationships vis-à-vis *senambele. Senambele* are no longer forbidden to observe Kulebele at work in areas where carvers are dependent upon the tourist art market for a livelihood and *senambele* Poro items are carved in the open, adjacent to public pathways. Kulebele no longer need to prevent *senambele* from learning the "secrets" of their craft for fear of competition for a limited market. The demands of the tourist art market are so great that Kulebele are often unable to meet them. For this reason they have begun to accept *senambele* as apprentices and instead of extracting food, livestock and money from *senambele* who see them carving, they now maximize their economic position by teaching *senambele* how to carve in exchange for labor and a six-and-one-half-year-long commitment to Kulebele Poro initiation which requires initiation fees of food, livestock and money.

Coping with Modernization

Although tourist art market participation has resulted in many changes in Kulebele social organization, some of which have resulted in conflict and stress, it has also been the means by which Kulebele have been able to respond positively to other sources of change. The razing of towns by the government and the requirements of purchasing a lot and building expensive houses have resulted in the emigration of poor families who lack the requisite financial resources. The poor move *en brousse* where mud-brick and thatch huts can still be built; only the relatively wealthy are able to remain in redeveloped towns. The annual per capita income in Ivory Coast was $350 in 1974 (*World Mark Encyclopedia of the Nations* 1976), but this figure includes the wealthier population in the South and Ivorian functionaries whose annual salaries are considerably higher than the yearly incomes of subsistence farmers. The annual per capita income is undoubtedly much less in the undeveloped northern part of the country. By contrast, the yearly earnings of Kulebele who are carving for the tourist art market range from a minimum of $384 to over $1500 (Richter 1978:325) and Kulebele who are tourist art market dealers and landlords realize a far greater annual income. Thus, because of their tourist art market earnings, Kulebele are able to comply with government schemes geared to development and are in the mainstream of modernization rather than relegated to areas where modernization has not yet been implemented.

Besides building modern homes, Kulebele have also been among the forerunners in the adoption of other status symbols emanating from the West such as motorbikes, electricity, tape recorders, radios, phonographs and watches. In 1974 three families had refrigerators and one bought a new television set. Many of these belongings serve only as status symbols, such as watches that virtually no one can read and refrigerators that only contain icewater because Kulebele believe that food stored in a refrigerator quickly spoils. However, other investments have allowed Kulebele to keep abreast with the concepts of modernization propagated and sometimes enforced by the government and some have resulted in an affirmation of "Kulebeleness"; as when the near-defunct Kolia Kulebele Poro was revitalized because migrant Kolia Kulebele in Korhogo earned enough money to buy motorbikes and to return to Kolia more frequently for Poro initiations and funerals. Motorbikes make it possible for Kulebele to participate in funerals in distant villages, and tourist art market earnings enable them to send women and children by public transport to distant villages where their kinsmen live. As a result, dispersed Kulebele interact more frequently today than in the past and *narigba7a* ties are more viable.

Kulebele have always been professional woodcarvers. Their motivation to carve has been economic rather than religious, with the exception of carving for their own Poro, which has constituted only a small fraction of their time and labor. Because the bulk of their carvings has always been produced for out-groups, the tourist art market simply expanded the market for their wares. Carving for the tourist market is not an innovative activity although it has resulted in changes not anticipated by Kulebele.

Without their specialized skills, for which there is much demand, Kulebele would number among the countless poor still engaged in a subsistence economy. However, as a result of the economic opportunities offered by the tourist art market, instead of being spectators in a modern world they are able to participate in it.

Changes in Esthetic Canons

The tourist art market has afforded the opportunity for men to carve who would not be carving in the traditional context. The items produced by them are not the result of deterioration of esthetic standards; their work is poor simply because they are not good carvers. The pressure of mass-production is not responsible for poor quality work.

Because carvers are now devoted to carving full-time, rather than executing only an occasional Poro or prestige object, techniques have improved and carvers are more expert with their tools than in the past. Face masks, such as *kpelie* carved for traditional use are now more delicately made and helmet masks, *kponyugu*,[85] are more intricately carved. Indeed, Kulebele maintain that they would no longer dance the older *kpelie* because they are heavy, tiring to dance and not as *kunyo* (good, beautiful) as newer masks. The difference between old and new *kpelie* can be seen in Plates 10 and 11, and is substantiated by measurements as shown in Table 3.

Table 3

	Thickness of mask 6 mm from the side	Thickness of side projections where they join the mask	Width eye-openings
1940 *kpelie*	6 mm	1.5 cm	4 mm
1976 *kpelie*	2.5 mm	1 cm	1 mm

Incising and bas-relief of details are other techniques that have become more delicately rendered as carvers become more adept with their tools. On the 1940 mask above, 10.5 mm are required for three welts beneath the eyes while only 7.5 mm are required for four welts on the new mask. Incising is used more freely on newer masks and statues of *ndebele* but only by master carvers engaged in tourist market production. Older men who once carved for the traditional market are often not able to incise with the straight, fine lines used by current master carvers. Carvers of lesser merit sometimes attempt fine-line incising but their efforts are not as precise. The tourist market has been responsible for greater facility with tools, resulting in refinements in detail in traditional objects.

A Note on the Future of Kulebele Carving

It is clear from the evidence presented in the preceding pages that Kulebele carving is flourishing and that master carvers produce good quality carvings for both the traditional and tourist art markets. They are encouraged and praised by fellow Kulebele and by the Senegalese and Hausa traders with whom they deal and who also reward them by paying them higher prices and giving them gifts. Kulebele dealers do not usually do business with master carvers for they are unwilling to pay the prices master carvers receive from foreign traders and they do not give gifts to carvers. Indeed, they often agree to a price, take possession of the carvings and do not pay in full, promising to complete payment at a later date, which they rarely do. Master carvers do not like to sell to Kulebele traders because they "cut men's throats." Inferior carvers, with whom Senegalese and Hausa traders do not do much business, deal almost exclusively with Kulebele traders who are the purveyors of most of the mass-produced, poor quality tourist carvings.

The Ivorian government is attempting to gain a monopoly over art objects produced in the country and claims it will sell at lower prices than Senegalese and Hausa dealers, which will result in more Ivorian art being sold. In order to obtain Kulebele carvings, the government appointed four wealthy Kulebele dealers as official agents for the procurement of Senufo carvings. At least one of these dealers shipped a large quantity of inferior carvings to the government in Abidjan. This occurred a few weeks before I left the field and gossip among the carvers was that the government had refused to accept the shipment because of the inferiority of the merchandise. Unfortunately, I left before I was able to substantiate the rumor.

It appears that two possible results are feasible with the involvement of the government in the tourist art market, both of which will negatively affect master carvers and the future quality of Kulebele carvings. If the government is successful in putting the Senegalese and Hausa dealers out of business, whom it perceives as competition, master carvers will be forced to deal with Kulebele traders who pay the lowest possible prices and frequently neglect to pay in full.

Master carvers state that they will not carve if they are not paid a price commensurate with their work and one master claims he will learn how to drive a car and become a chauffeur, by which he would earn more money than if he carved for Kulebele dealers. Dealing with Kulebele traders also results in constant irritation and tension because they do not pay the price they agree to. Another master stated that "my heart is not happy" when he works for Kulebele traders, therefore he does not do as good work for them. It appears that being forced to deal with Kulebele traders will result in master carvers seeking work other than carving or not producing the high quality carvings they provide foreign dealers.

The government is attempting to control the quality of carvings it sells to tourists, and government rejection of poor quality carvings will close the tourist market to inferior carvers. On the other hand, by dealing through Kulebele traders, master carvers will be discouraged from participating, except on the level of poorer quality. It seems likely that second category carvers, those who are skilled craftsmen with small repertoires and who are often influenced by non-traditional motifs, will provide the bulk of carvings produced for the government and sold to the outside world.

Notes

Introduction

1 See Bascom (1976) for a historical perspective on western judgments on the demise of African art.

2 See also Abramson (1970:54) and Carroll (1961).

3 See also Bravmann (1974:83-84) on carvers in eastern Ivory Coast and western Ghana; Brain and Pollock (1971:39) on Bangway carvers; and Thoret (1971) on blacksmiths, potters and weavers in Ivory Coast.

4 See also Ames (1962:47-48), Bravmann (1974:83), Hodder and Ukwu (1969:16-17, 121-122), Lloyd (1953), Nadel (1969:264, 270 and 283) and Thoret (1971).

5 See also Abramson (1970:55), d'Azevedo (1970:3), Bascom (1973a:66) and Fernandez (1973:198).

6 See also d'Azevedo (1970:63), Graburn (1969:7) and Ryerson (1976:128).

7 See also Atamian (1966), Furst (1968-9:21) and Stromberg (1976).

8 Graburn (1976b:1) describes the Fourth World as:
 . . . all aboriginal or native people whose lands fall within the national boundaries and technobureaucratic administrations of the countries of the First, Second and Third Worlds. As such, they are peoples without countries of their own, peoples who are usually in the minority and without power to direct the course of their collective lives.
 See Crowley (1977:8) for comments on Graburn's definition.

9 See also Brody (1976:73) and Kent (1976:86-91).

10 See d'Azevedo (1970:63).

11 See also Lathrap (1976:202 and 204) re Shipibo-Conibo potters and Williams (1976:269-70) re bark painters at Yirrkala.

Chapter 1: Kulebeleland: Physical and Social Environments

12 Glaze (1976:122) argues that "men's society" is a misnomer because women play an important role in them. She suggests using the term "village society" which more accurately reflects a wider participation.

13 Person (1973b:272) defines Dyula as "commerçants la plupart d'origine mandique ou sarakole."

14 Fulani are pastoral Muslims who are scattered over the savanna of the western Sudan from Senegambia to the Central African Republic. See Stenning (1959).

15 Ivory Coast is divided into geographical areas called *préfectures* which are governed by *préfets.* Within each *préfecture* are several *sous-préfectures,* each of which is headed by a *sous-préfet.*

16 See Person (1970:Vol.II) for a complete history of Samori's eastern campaigns.

17 This statement is based upon genealogies collected during the fieldwork. See Richter (in press) for a detailed discussion on "castes" in Senufoland.

18 Lorho is Dyula for the brasscasters' *fijio.* Brasscasters are called Kpeembele by Senari-speakers.

19 This is in error. Kpeembele are brasscasters.

20 The stress is on the second syllables of Kulebele and Guleo.

21 The figure 190 is based upon information provided by the Kulebele chief at San, who is in his mid-70's, plus four generations of 30 years each. Kulebele did not, in the past, marry until they were in their 30's and sometimes, their early 40's.

22 According to Fonombele oral tradition, they too were unmolested during times of war because their skills were highly desired by all belligerants.

23 The Dyula are accused by Senufo and non-Senufo, e.g., Hausa, of being isolationists and inhospitable. "Wherever you find a lot of Dyula, the village will never grow." In fact, this is not true. Two of the largest villages in northern Ivory Coast, Kouto and Kolia, had Dyula chiefs and sizeable Dyula populations at the turn of the century (see Delafosse [1908a] and *Statistique administratif, ethnique et économique* [1908]).

24 A concession is a spatial area usually headed by an adult male and inhabited by individuals who identify themselves as members of a socially definable group bound together by kinship or common interest.

25 With the exception of the population figures for Korhogo, Bolpe and Kanono 2, all census figures are based on a 1963 census published by the Ministère du Plan (1973). A census was made by the Ivorian government in 1975 but the figures were not available by the time I left Ivory Coast. According to an unpublished World Bank report (1972) the population of Korhogo in 1970 was 32,000 and was increasing at the rate of 5.9% per year. The population figures for Bolpe and Kanono 2 are based on censuses I made during the fieldwork.

26 I never encountered a case where permission was denied.

27 See Gardi (1973:153) for a schematic of a Senufo village.

28 See Thoret (1971) for a description of how foreign artisans settled in southeastern Senufoland.

Chapter 2: Kinship and Family Organization

29 A full analysis of kinship is beyond the scope of this monograph, neither is it necessary to its aims. The partial analysis which follows is intended to point out a few of the anomalies that indicate the weakening of the matrilineage in matters of inheritance, a significant feature of the social organization which integrates with an increase in the economic power of individuals. See Colson (1962:72-73), Fortes (1949:65-82), Gough (1962:631-654) and Turner (1957:133-136 and 218-221) for discussions on kinship and economic individualization.

30 Jamin (1973:30) states that *jao* is a term used only for sons among the Kiembara Senufo. Keintz (1975) does not substantiate this in his research among the Kiembara or do my data for Kulebele. Jamin's diagram of Kiembara kinship relations (Jamin 1973:fig.3) inaccurately illustrates the *narigba7a* inasmuch as he includes Ego's brothers' children and sisters' sons' children in it. Kientz's data substantiate mine.

31 The parentage of these two couples was checked with several informants who also stated that half-siblings could marry under the above conditions, but I am not comfortable with the data. Western Kulebele speak a dialect I neither speak nor understand easily. Although one informant from the area also spoke Dalir, French and some English and another also spoke Dalir and French, the possibility exists that I was not successful in weeding out "true father" from "father-in-general," although I was able to do so in other cases that had more complete genealogies. While I checked and rechecked this information and ultimately accepted its validity while I was in the field, I found it difficult to accept once I had returned to the States. Undoubtedly, my own cultural biases are showing which were exacerbated by eastern Kulebele disgust and astonishment when I asked them about their attitudes about half-sibling unions and the fact that no marriage of this type was recorded among eastern Kulebele. In any event, I feel that this information needs to be checked further.

32 Contiguous *kacoli* of particular ethnic groups are also destroyed by road-building programs. Kulebele in Kolia had their own quarter which consisted of three adjacent *kacoli.* When the new road was constructed from Boundiali to Tengrila, it cut through the center of Kolia, destroying many quarters. The village was ultimately laid out in a grid pattern and the various ethnic groups are now thoroughly integrated spatially. At present, Kulebele in Kolia are organized in the original three *kacoli,* but they are located in three different parts of town.

While the government sets down the regulations concerned with "modernization," how quickly they are complied with depends upon the zeal of individual *sous-préfets* and *préfets* (see note 15). The seats of the *préfectures* are the first to be modernized; those of *sous-préfectures* are second. Villages *en brousse* are the last to be affected. *Sous-préfets* impose arbitrary time limits in which house-construction must begin after purchase of the lot, e.g., the *sous-préfet* of Korhogo insists that all house walls must be raised within three months after purchase of a lot, though as of the end of 1975 he had not imposed any time limits for finishing construction. In contrast, the *sous-préfet* of Kolia, a newly designated *sous-préfecture,*has allowed a year for house walls to be finished. Kulebele in Kolia who do not already live in concrete-block houses are buying cement and having concrete blocks made as they can afford it. Once all the necessary concrete blocks are finished and enough money has been saved to pay for labor, they will have the walls raised. In other villages, the *sous-préfets* simply insist on corrugated-metal roofs in lieu of the traditional thatch which is a serious fire hazard, but they are not concerned with mud-brick walls. The need to pay 5,000 CFA for a lot and to build a concrete-block house, which cost approximately $2,000 in 1975, often forces villagers to move to a village where modernization has not yet been enforced and traditional mud-brick and thatch huts can still be built.

33 Ingyams are starchy tubers, of which there are numerous varieties.

Chapter 3: Political Organization and Poro

34 Poro is the singular and plural form. Not all secret societies in Senufoland are Poro. For example, the Wambele is a secret society that originated with the Nafana, a *senambele* group east and south of Korhogo. Membership in Wambele is voluntary; membership in Poro is obligatory. The Nafana also have Poro.

35 See Bochet (1959), Clamens (1955), Glaze (1976), Holas (1966:146-152), Jamin (1973:9-11) and Knops (1959:92-95) for detailed descriptions of various Poro.

36 I was not able to elicit the names used for the drums, which are sacred objects, as opposed to flutes, rasps and rattles, which are secular. The power of the drums is greatly feared by Kulebele and non-Kulebele although restrictions surrounding their use and handling vary from one Kulebele Poro to the next. For example, women are not allowed to touch the Korhogo or Danebolo Poro drums, but Kulebele teenage girls in Kolia are very casual about the Kolia Kulebele Poro drums, which they lean on and against and sit upon with impunity. A Celo informant implied that Kulebele hid human genitals inside their drums, which were the source of their power. A

132

surreptitious inspection of the inside of one of the large Kulebele drums revealed small wads of cotton concealed within.

37 The second age grade of the Korhogo Poro tried to convince their *kafu* to allow them to transport their drums, masks and costumes in my car to a funeral that was 125 kilometers distant, but he would not allow it. Poro funeral gear and masquerades are allegedly transported by supernatural means from one place to another and non-initiates—particularly women—should not see them being transported. *Senambele* in the Korhogo area still transport Poro baggage by headloading and on foot and women are warned of their impending approach by a specific drumbeat and the sounding of an iron bell. Women hide in their huts when they hear Poro approaching. Kulebele are not as rigid about women seeing their Poro equipment disassembled or masqueraders unmasked, but they transport their gear as unobtrusively as possible, which would not have been possible in an automobile which always draws crowds of curious women and children. Also, the fact that I was an uninitiated female may have had some bearing on the decision.

Many Senufo groups will not allow pre-menopausal women to observe certain categories of masks dance or parade, which often occur in public places. Women must hide and not look at these activities or they will be killed by the powers of the Poro. Kulebele are not concerned if their women see the Poro activities of other Poro: they maintain that Kulebele women are impervious to the negative supernatural sanctions of other Poro. However, the *senambele* Poro in Korhogo are policed by club-wielding maskers *(yelejɔgɔ)* who threaten and physically abuse non-initiates in public places where particular Poro activities are taking place. For this reason, Kulebele women generally comply with the interdiction against viewing activities proscribed for women by the *senambele* Poro.

While non-*senambele* women fear *senambele* Poro, they do not take it too seriously when their own initiates are concerned. I have seen a Fonon initiate of one of the *senambele* Poro headload his costume and club into his *kacolo* when it was full of pre-menopausal Fonombele women, which is prohibited by *senambele*. The women laughed and pointed at the young man who simply responded with a withering glance, which resulted in more laughter. In this case *senambele* Poro ethics were broken by both the Fonon initiate, who failed to announce his approach and who entered an area full of pre-menopausal women, and the women, who did not hide when they became aware of his presence.

Strangers or people disliked by Kulebele are chased away from public funeral ceremonies by threat of a beating with the braided leather quirts carried by the second age grade. Kulebele women and children are free to watch Kulebele masks dance in public. Indeed, the calabash rattle *(celo)* that is part of the Kulebele orchestra accompanying masked dancers is owned by women and is played by a young woman.

38 I have no idea what part elders play in initiations which are carried out in the sacred grove *(sinzang).* The *sinzang* was closed to me as a westerner and a woman and all business conducted in it was considered Poro secrets not to be shared with non-initiates. Further, Kulebele were concerned that I might divulge Poro secrets, i.e., write about them. While they were willing to discuss non-Kulebele Poro, they did not want their secrets recorded or discussed. They have seen books with photographs of Poro masks, and postcards of *senambele* maskers are on sale in the bookstores in Korhogo and displayed in windows and there is a large tourist poster of Wambele maskers in the hotel. Kulebele are scandalized that other Poro allow their activities to be known: Poro activities should not be made public. See Glaze (1975 and 1976) for Kufulo women's role in Poro.

At present there is a strict prohibition by the Poro against taking photos of any maskers in Korhogo, the result of the publishing of pictures that have been taken in the past. The Poro whose maskers appear on postcards, in books and on travel posters are very unhappy about the situation. The main concern is that Poro secrets—supernatural powers—can be learned by observing photos or reading about rituals, and such information, when in the hands of an adversary, might be used against the Poro depicted or described. Since Kulebele have seen depictions of other Poro maskers made public, they have begun to carve them in bas-relief on doors for the tourist art market, though they do not depict their own maskers. Their depictions are detailed and completely accurate; they even include the appropriate musicians and musical instruments that accompany the masker.

39 Djemtana is Himmelheber's Fudansrugu (Himmelheber 1960:96).

40 There are several categories of individuals in Senufoland who control supernatural powers, all of which are glossed "sorcerer" by French-speaking Senufo. A discussion of these categories is not relevant within the context of this study and the term "sorcerer" will suffice.

41 The *narobele* of the Korhogo Kulebele *kafu* clearly feared *senambele* Poro and on one occasion walked half a mile into the bush to avoid contact with *senambele* Poro maskers and remained there for the better part of an hour until the maskers departed. Non-Muslim Kulebele never reacted in this manner to *senambele* Poro. The *narobele* would not explain their fear of *senambele* Poro to me, but the following facts may be pertinent. These *narobele* were among the first Senufo to deal in antique woodcarvings, which they sold to French administrators. While they would not sell antique Kulebele masks and carvings to the French, they did deal in *senambele* antiques. Indeed, their current wealth is based upon their earlier dealings in antique *senambele* carvings. According to a Hausa informant who was born and raised in

Korhogo, whose father dealt in antique carvings and who deals in them himself, Kulebele stole many of the carvings they sold to the French. Because they were called upon to carve for *senambele* and often had access to *senambele sinzang,* they were aware of what was secreted there and would return and steal sacred Poro carvings. If this is true and the *narobele* mentioned above were participants, their fear of *senambele* Poro is understandable. Even though the Poro members may not know the identity of the thieves, the supernatural powers of Poro would ferret them out.

42 Holas (1960:51) states that Kafigelejo is a Senufo "fetish," but, in fact, it is uniquely Kulebele. He states that it is found among the Kufulo, who are in the Dikodougou area, as well as among several other groups. Glaze (1977) states she did not hear of Kafigelejo during the 18 months she lived among the Kufulo. Kulebele insist that Kafigelejo is used only by them.

Chapter 4: Traditional Artists and Tourist Art

43 Adzes and carving knives are not perceived as potential weapons by children. Not once, in two-and-one-half years, did I see a child brandish a carving tool as a weapon.

44 See Chapter 5 for details on *senambele*/Kulebele relationships.

45 Kulebele claim that on occasion a good carver was killed by *senambele* Poro after he had executed a particularly fine mask, to insure that it would not be duplicated for another Poro.

46 In the Dikodougou area where Kulebele are involved only with the tourist art market, approximately 400 to 500 masks per month are produced.

47 Prices are not generally discussed among Kulebele; they are estimated by the category of dealers who buy one's work. In reality, prices are generally known by other carvers.

Chapter 5: Migration

48 The Kulebele elders in Tiogo do not know from whence they originated. However, the Kulebele *kafu* at San claims that Tiogo Kulebele emigrated from *San.*

49 "Behind" in this context means that their village origin was north or east of Kouto.

50 See Person 1971.

51 See letter from Post du Segoumo to the Chef du Cercle (May 16, 1914) in which the "Koules" are referred to as "charpentiers."

The French policy of conscripted labor in colonial West Africa was implemented early in the 20th century and continued until 1945. Conscripts were used to do plantation work, for work in the timber industry, on roads and railroads and, in Ivory Coast, at the wharf at Grand Bassam. Examples of the numbers of men involved in forced labor can be found in the Rapport Annuel Sur Le Travail (1938), which notes a total of 49,993 conscripts officially employed in 1937, and 46,973 in 1938. While most conscripts were engaged on government projects, Kulebele were often impressed to carve for administrators for personal reasons, i.e., on unofficial projects. At least one of the masks in the Musée d'Abidjan (Holas 1969:plate 101) was carved under this policy.

52 The focus in this section and the next will be on Kulebele who depend upon carving to supplement their farming and not on Kulebele who do little carving and depend upon farming.

53 A village to which Kulebele migrate and which is not considered by them to be a traditional Kulebele village will be called a "host-village."

54 Payment was in cowries, livestock and food.

55 A Guleo's competency as a carver determines what items he carves. Carvers who have not completed Poro initiation can and do carve ritual objects within the range of their abilities. A carver's standing within the Poro is not relevant to the commissions he receives. One highly admired carver publicly renounced Poro and refused to participate further in Poro activities once he had been fully initiated, but he is still sought out to carve masks for various Poro.

56 Many of the woodcarvings in the tourist art market are carved by teenagers who are still in the process of learning to carve and of polishing their technique. They have a limited repertoire.

Chapter 6: Exploitation of Supernatural Sanctions

57 See also Bascom (1976:307), Biebuyck (1976), Carroll (1961:21) and Raum (1961:10).

58 See Vaughan (1970) for a listing of West African societies in which artisan groups are found.

59 But not considered inferior as propounded by Knops (1959:91).

60 See Goldwater (1964:illustrations 142-144) and Holas (1966:plate 59). See Note 42.

61 Kulebele men and boys eat Kafigelejo sacrifices with pleasure and without fear. Non-Kulebele politely refuse them, much to the amusement of Kulebele. Indeed, if Kulebele men do not want to share non-sacrificial meat with strangers (any non-Kulebele) they offer a portion of meat, in keeping with the ideals of hospitality, while stating it is meat of the Kafigelejo. The invitation to eat is inevitably refused.

62 It can be argued that by not imposing Kafigelejo sanctions, inner-group conflict is avoided, but this is not the case since major inner-group conflicts do occur regularly with varying degrees of severity. The purpose of avoiding inter-Kafigelejo conflicts is to prevent the untenable situation of Kafigelejo being used against itself, i.e., $Kafigelejo_1$ in conflict with $Kafigelejo_2$ both of which are Kafigelejo.

63 This is beginning to change when a prospective son-in-law is well-employed. Indeed, one Kulebele elder sought out and was successful in marrying one of his female dependents to a non-Kulebele minor functionary who had an automobile, a status symbol indicating considerable wealth.

64 Middle-aged *senambele* informant.

65 This is estimated to have occurred approximately 25 years ago, based on Kulebele chief lists, oral tradition and genealogies.

66 "African medicine doesn't work against whites," stated a Kulebele elder.

67 Approximately $250.

68 An example of fear of negative supernatural sanctions being brought to bear on civil servants of other ethnic groups is evinced in a case of three American Peace Corps volunteers, two young men and a young woman, taking photographs at a Poro funeral and being caught by members of one of the participating Poro. Taking photographs of masked dancers at funerals is strictly forbidden in Korhogo and environs. Masked Poro initiates confiscated both of the volunteers' cameras. The volunteers were also pushed about, verbally abused and the girl's dress was torn during the fracas. They were able to recover one camera by appealing to a highly placed government official who was also an important elder in the Poro sponsoring the funeral. The volunteers attempted to make a police report concerning the other camera but had great difficulty finding policemen willing to take the report for fear of supernatural Poro sanctions. After three days of appealing to police officials, they were finally successful in making a report, but never recovered their camera. Most of the police officials were neither from Korhogo nor Senufo, but they were very aware of Poro powers. It should be noted that all three of the Peace Corps volunteers were aware of the prohibition of taking photographs at funerals.

69 Larger-scale tree-felling is done with heavy motorized equipment with which Kulebele are not familiar.

70 Ideally, non-initiates should not see particular species of Poro masks dance but, in fact, many do from a distance. The trick is to observe without drawing attention to oneself. Farmer Senufo do not allow women to see some of their masks dance under any circumstances unless they are foreigners. While Kulebele are not concerned if their women see these masks, the farmers are, and impose their own sanctions. Kulebele claim the farmers' masks themselves cannot affect

Kulebele women but the farmers' other supernatural and physical sanctions, such as whipping and beating, are recognized as dangerous.

71 See Bochet (1959:figure 3 bottom).

Chapter 7: Exploitation of New Economic Opportunities

72 In 1975, a small cow cost 20,000 CFA which is roughly $100. In Korhogo in 1974-1975, cowries were exchanged for francs at the rate of five cowries per franc.

73 A Dutch agricultural volunteer supplied the information on problems of keeping cattle in Senufoland.

74 The man who made this statement is a member of a *senambele* Poro as well as two Kulebele Poro.

75 See Zemp (1965) for an illustration of these trumpets. Bas-relief is not traditional on musical instruments. The trader who owned the trumpets believed they would be more readily saleable if they had designs carved in bas-relief. A similar phenomenon is occurring with old, plain doors which the traders buy *en brousse* and take to Kulebele to be carved in bas-relief. The decoration is new, though the doors are old and are sold as antiques.

76 Allison (1963:130) notes a similar phenomenon in Nigeria where a family of woodcarvers and another of brasscasters regularly trade new objects for old which they then sell.

77 This ideal is far from being realized. I have seen Baule-style masks carved and shipped to government agencies by Kulebele and observed a Guleo and four other carvers from other ethnic groups at the atélier in Grand Bassam employed at carving turtles of questionable origin for the government.

78 This is, they pay approximately $7.50 to $12.50 per drum and retail them for $50 or higher.

Chapter 8: Summary and Conclusion

79 See Pearson (1973b:107) and Collieaux (1924).

80 See Pearson (1973a:216).

81 These data were extrapolated from Fiches signaletiques des chefs indigenes (1918-1926).

82 Clignet (1966) found that urban matrilineal Aboure and patrilineal Bete, both of whom are forest peoples in Ivory Coast, married later than in rural areas, which is in contrast to the Senufo pattern.

83 See Note 29.

84 The diet of Kulebele in the East is one of the poorest in Senufoland in terms of variety and animal protein. The only way that it differs from

the diet of poor and rural *senambele* is that there is usually more of it, though one chiefly Kulebele lineage is so poor that it subsisted at a near-starvation level the entire time I was in Korhogo; the daily intake of the one remaining wife, who was nursing an infant, and her five other children often consisted of three or four small pieces of boiled ingyam for each without seasoning or sauce at noon and less than a cup of *to7* in a watery vegetable sauce at night. Most Kulebele children manifest evidence of kwashiorkor (distended bellies, stick arms and legs and swollen joints) until they are approximately ten years old, though the eldest child of the impoverished lineage mentioned above still manifested these symptoms in his mid-teens.

In 1974 the two-year-old daughter of a wealthy Kulebele *kafu* died of malnutrition and dehydration according to hospital records. The management of this child's health problems is a vivid example of the misunderstandings that arise when indigenous peoples encounter western beliefs about the relationship between diet and health and western-trained health practitioners do not fully understand indigenous culture. The child's mother took her to an American missionary health clinic several miles south of Korhogo six weeks before she died. The missionary diagnosed malnutrition and dehydration in its early stages. Aware that animal protein is not fed to small children, she prescribed that the child be fed millet gruel which, according to the missionary, is more nourishing and has a higher protein content than corn gruel. However, millet is a low-status food and the child was the daughter of a wealthy high-status chief who was insulted and disgusted by the suggestion that millet be fed to any of his dependents. The child's mother also felt insulted and was upset that the child was not given an injection which, she believed, would have cured her. The missionary's advice was not heeded and the child was fed corn gruel which she did not like and ate little of and mangos which she did like and ate willingly. She was also nursing although almost weaned.

Six weeks later, after indigenous remedies failed and it became obvious that the child was severely ill she was taken to the hospital in Korhogo where she was admitted in acute distress. A hospital attendant gave the mother a thick gruel and a spoon and told her to feed the child. The child rejected the spoon—she had no experience with a spoon—and the mother would not feed her with her fingers for fear of being considered backward and uncouth. The child died during the night. Although it is doubtful that food earlier in the evening would have prevented her death, the misunderstanding between the mother and the hospital attendant clearly signals a significant problem as does the lack of understanding between the mother and the missionary.

While meat is infrequently eaten by Kulebele women and children, men eat it almost daily. They purchase grilled fish and meat for their own consumption away from home and out of sight of their families. One such instance involved a wealthy Guleo *kacolofolo* who purchased two grilled half-chickens, one of which he consumed on the spot, the other of which he took home to be shared by four adult women and five children. Men also eat the boiled meat of animal sacrifices to Kafigelejo which they share with male children but this source of meat is forbidden to females. They also eat the meat of small livestock and fowls that constitute a part of Poro initiates' fees, which is also forbidden to non-initiates, which include women and children. Meat connected with Poro activities is available only during the dry season, when Poro activities are the most intense. Animals are butchered at funerals but by the time the meat has been distributed to the many guests, individual portions often consist of little more than a bite or two.

Kulebele do not ordinarily buy milk although they value it and consider it a prestige food to be reserved for men and honored guests. The only times I saw milk consumed by Kulebele were two occasions *en brousse* when it was purchased to honor my visit. Kulebele collect chicken and guinea-fowl eggs to sell, but I encountered only one person who ate eggs and she was a *senao* married to a Guleo. She was a wealthy market woman who could afford to indulge herself. Her two young daughters were the healthiest-appearing children among the Kulebele. Two of her husband's sons by another wife (deceased) who lived in the same household appeared to be suffering from kwashiorkor.

Increased male income does not lead to a better diet for Kulebele women and children. In contrast, wealthy *senambele* in Korhogo provide meat for their wives and children almost daily and rice, which is more expensive than corn and is considered a prestige food, is eaten at least once each day. The children of Korhogo Fonombele, who are generally very poor unless they give up blacksmithing for more lucrative work, appear healthier than Kulebele children. The Fonombele diet is frugal in terms of quantity, but it includes meat at least once a week, of which the children are given relatively generous portions. Whereas many Fonombele children appear sickly and suffering from kwashiorkor, their symptoms do not appear to be as severe as those of Kulebele children. Also, Fonombele children have glossier skins and happier dispositions than Kulebele children, whose skin is dry, cracked and ashy and who are often listless, irritable and cry a great deal.

85 *Kponyugu* is the generic term for helmet mask. The *kponyugu* in Plate 9 is a *wanugu* which is danced by the Wambele society which is a sorcerer's secret society found primarily among the Nafambele who are farmers living east and southeast of Korhogo. All of the helmet masks in Figure 2 in Bochet (1965) are *kponyugu* as he points out. See Richter (1979).

Glossary

barapipiu (sing.); barapipibele (pl.): apprentice.

-bele: plural suffix.

fijiɔ (sing.); fijembele (pl.): group identified with an occupation other than farming, member of such a group.

-gele: plural suffix.

Guleo: singular of Kulebele.

jao (sing.); jabele (pl.): child, dependent.

jatugu (sing.): patron or sponsor of strangers.

ka7a (sing.): village, quarter in a village.

ka7afolo (sing.): "owner" of the ka7a, chief of the ka7a.

kafu (sing.); kafubele (pl.): chief of a ka7a.

kacana: good luck.

kacolo (sing.); kacoli (pl.): residential unit.

kacolofolo (sing.): head of a kacolo.

kapele: bad luck.

kpa7a (sing.): hut, house.

Kolocelo: supreme diety and creator god.

kponyugu (sing.): generic term for helmet mask.

kulyeebe (sing.); kulyeebele (pl.): ancestor.

kunyo: good, beautiful in a physical or moral sense; winyo when applied to a person.

narjao (sing.): female member of the narigba7a.

narigba7a (sing.); narigbaya (pl.): the matrilineage.

narigbafolo (sing.): "owner" of the narigba7a, chief of the narigba7a.

naro (sing.); narobele (pl.): sister's son or daughter.

ndao (sing.); ndebele (pl.): non-human spirits that live in natural features of the land, bush spirits.

nojao (sing.); nojabele (pl.): male child, son, male dependent.

nubu (sing.); nubombele (pl.): stranger, foreigner.

nyeneya7asa7a (sing.): father's narigba7a.

pil (sing.); pigele (pl.): "soul."

piu (sing.); pibele (pl.): child, dependent.

Poro (sing. and pl.): village society in which male membership is obligatory and females are excluded from initiation until post-menopausal.

senao (sing.); senambele (pl.): group identified with farming as an occupation, member of such a group.

sheleo (sing.): mother's brother.

sinzang (sing.): sacred Poro forest.

tamofo (sing.): one who knows, "master."

Comments on the Plates

1   Main concentration of Kulebele in Korhogo; Kulebele *kacolobele* are outlined. The stand of mango trees within the outline shades the area where Kulebele carve and have their work sheds *(bugupile)*. The thatched huts north of the mangoes are the dwellings in Plate 3. The large stand of trees in the lower right quarter is a *sinzang*. The western portion is used by a *senambele* Poro and the eastern portion is used by Danebolo and Korhogo Kulebele Poro. The tall deciduous trees in the *sinzang* are bombax (kapok) trees the thorn of which is represented on the crest of some *kpelie* masks (Richter 1979:73). The large unfinished building top center is a new mosque. The building above it is the old mosque. The large shed in the upper right-hand corner is where the evening food market is held. The dense mud-brick and thatch residential area in the upper left was razed in 1975. The downtown area of Korhogo, which includes the main market, shops, banks and government offices is two blocks to the East.

2   Market day in Tyoronyaradougou, 12 miles south of Korhogo. This market is an important one and draws participants from considerable distances, many of whom arrive in public buses. It is not frequented by tourists or resident Europeans in Korhogo and the goods that are sold in the market are for the consumption of local people. Tyoronyaradougou is a pottery center where pots are made in anticipation of sales in the local market. Potters also headload their pots to Korhogo to sell on the big market day there. The cloths in this photo were woven in Senufoland though not in Tyoronyaradougou. They are brought to market by the weavers who made them or by middlemen and are also sold in the Korhogo market. Fonombele women have a large display and wide selection of baskets and trays in this market as do blacksmiths, some of whom reside and work in Korhogo and other villages and travel from one market to another peddling their products. Jelebele and Kpeembele are often found in the markets displaying their wares. There is a Jelebele work area adjacent to the Korhogo market site where they work every day and where their ready-made leather goods such as sandals, knife sheaths and ceremonial whisks are displayed and special orders can be commissioned.

3   The Kulebele work area in Quartier Koko is a remnant of the Korhogo Kulebele chief's original *kacolo* located beneath the mango trees in Plate 1. In 1976 the *sous-préfet* of Korhogo ordered that the huts in the background be razed. The hut on the extreme right was occupied by an

143

elder who is second in line to the Danebolo Kulebele chieftainship and indicates the level of poverty of the Danebolo *narigba7a.* The other huts are occupied by women. The workshed *(bugupile)* in the center is used by teenage boys. Note the statues mass-produced by one of the teenagers for the tourist art market.

4   Concrete-block houses built by Kulebele after Quartier Koko was razed in the mid-1960's. The Kulebele work area is in the foreground.

5   Carving knives. The knife on the right is older than the other three and the blade is worn down.

6   Zie Coulibaly using a carving knife. The knife is also held with the blade away from the wrist, depending upon the area being carved.

7   Carving adzes. Note the differences in the length and width of the blades. Heavier and wider blades are used for roughing-out carvings. Lighter and narrower blades are used for finer work. The stubby wooden tool upon which the blades are resting is a mallet used to drive the knife blade into wood when outlining bas-relief designs.

8   Diseliba Coulibaly roughing-out a mask. His adze stroke is at its apex. Roughing-out a carving at arm's length is the characteristic manner of handling work at this stage.

9   Wanugu carved by master carver Ngolo Coulibaly who migrated from Bolpe to Korhogo when he was a boy. This helmet mask was commissioned by a member of Wambele, a secret initiation society found primarily among the Nafambele who are located east of Korhogo. *Wa:* sting, pierce; *nugu:* head. Wambele are noted for their ability to use bees as messengers carrying sickness or death to specific victims. Wambele is a voluntary society, not compulsory as is Poro. Approximately 37 inches in length.

10   *Kpelie* carved by Ngolo Coulibaly (Kolia) in 1976, commissioned by the author. This mask is Poro quality and is the type currently being carved for Poro by master carvers who also carve for the tourist art market. 12½ inches in height.

11   *Kpelie* carved by Liyerege (Dabakaha) and danced by the Dabakaha Kulebele Poro from the early 1940's until 1975. Liyerege was a master carver who did not carve for the tourist art market. 14½ inches in height.

12   Wanugu commissioned by this writer from Ngolo Coulibaly (Plate 9). A traditional Wanugu would not be incised after staining so that the

144

natural color of the wood would show through, a technique used on traditional chiefs' chairs. Although the carvers apply black and red colors to masks, mask owners apply white in spots and various other patterns and designs. The incising on this mask was an afterthought. The mask was completed the morning of a rainy day and the carver was not inspired to begin a new project. He was relaxing and admiring his mask and began incising the horns in an off-handed "doodling" manner. Pleased with the initial results he incised the chameleons, bird and cup. His innovation was admired and discussed by other carvers, some of whom left their work to greet Ngolo and inspect the mask. 37 inches in length.

13 Tourist art market masks carved by Tchekundjie Coulibaly inspired by Baule, Yaoure and Guro masks he had seen when he lived in Abidjan briefly. Approximately 17 inches in height.

14 Tourist art market masks produced in Nafoun that are bought and sold for cheap prices because they do not meet Kulebele esthetic standards. The center mask lacks depth, has both Baule and Senufo features, is too heavy and the mask and its components are not well formed. The two flanking masks are too heavy, the incising is poorly executed and the appendages are not well formed. Approximately 14 inches in height.

15 Kulebele quarter at Sumo. The rectangular thatched mud-brick dwellings were built by young men out of tourist art market earnings and are modelled on concrete-block houses built in Korhogo.

16 Korhogo Kulebele *kafu*, in the dark garment, inspecting his cattle at Sumo. All of these cattle belong to Kulebele; eight of them belong to the Korhogo Kulebele *kafu* who had ten animals in this herd but two had disappeared. The *kafu* did not keep all of his cattle in this herd. His cattle were scattered widely in various villages, which was a means of disguising his full cattle wealth which, if it were blatantly apparent, might attract attention and arouse jealousy and negative supernatural sanctions. Scattering cattle among several herds over a wide area also protects the owner should disease decimate one herd. The man in the background is the Fulani herdsman who lives in the Kulebele quarter in Sumo with his wives and children and cares for the Kulebele herd there.

17 A new complex of houses for rental purposes built by the Korhogo Kulebele *kafu*. Some of the capital used to build these units came from selling cattle. The choice of arrangement and type of units maximize rentable living space within government building regulations. When further funds are available one or two more row-type apartment buildings will be added on the left.

18 The dependents of a wealthy Guleo staining mass-produced tourist art market masks purchased in the Dikodougou area.

145

Bibliography

Abramson, J. A. The Third Awam Style. *Artforum* 9:3:54-57, 1970.

Allison, P. K. Collecting for Nigeria's Museums. *Nigeria* 77:125-130, 1963.

Ames, David. The Rural Wolof of the Gambia. In *Markets in Africa*. Paul Bohannon and George Dalton, eds. Evanston: Northwestern University Press, 1962.

Angouvant, Gabriel. Letter to the Gouverneur Général de l'Afrique Occidental Française. Archive Nationale de la Côte d'Ivoire (ANCI) 1EE7(3), 1908.

_____. Arrêté. ANCI 1EE(79)1, February 15, 1913.

Atamian, Sarkis. The Anaktuvuk Mask and Cultural Innovation. *Science* 151:3716:1337-1345, 1966.

Barnett, Homer. *Innovation: The Basis of Culture Change*. New York: McGraw-Hill, 1953.

Barth, F. Economic Spheres in Darfur. In *Themes in Economic Anthropology*. R. Firth, ed. ASA Monograph #6. London: Tavistock, 1967.

Barth, Heinrich. *Travels and Discoveries in North and Central Africa*. London: Frank Cass & Co., 1965. Originally published by Longmans Green & Co., 1857.

Bascom, William. A Yoruba Master Carver: Duga of Meko. In *The Traditional Artist in African Societies*. Warren d'Azevedo, ed. Bloomington: Indiana University Press, 1973a.

_____. *African Art in Cultural Perspective*. New York: W. W. Norton, 1973b.

Beinart, Julian. *The Popular Art of Africa*. Johannesburg: Institute for the Study of Man, 1965.

Ben-Amos, Paula. "A La Recherche du Temps Perdu": On Being an Ebony-Carver in Benin. In *Ethnic and Tourist Arts*. Nelson Graburn, ed. Berkeley: University of California Press, 1976.

Berreman, Gerald. Caste in India and the United States. *American Journal of Sociology* 65:120-127, 1960.

Biebuyck, Daniel P. The Decline of Lega Sculpture. In *Ethnic and Tourist Arts*. Nelson Graburn, ed. Berkeley: University of California Press, 1976.

Boahen, A. Adu. The Caravan Trade in the Nineteenth Century. In *Problems in African History*. Robert O. Collins, ed. Englewood Cliffs: Prentice-Hall, 1968.

Bochet, Gilbert. Le poro des Dieli. *Bulletin de l'Institute Fondamental d'Afrique Noire* (Series B) 21:1-2:61-101, 1959.

_____. Les Masques sénoufo, de la forme à la signification. *Bulletin de l'Institut Fondamental d'Afrique Noire* (Series B) 27:3-4:636-677, 1965.

Brain, Robert and Pollock, Adam. *Bangwa Funerary Sculpture.* Toronto: University of Toronto Press, 1971.

Bravmann, Rene A. *Islam and Tribal Art in West Africa.* London: Cambridge University Press, 1974.

Brody, J. J. The Creative Consumer: Survival, Revival and Invention in Southwest Indian Arts. In *Ethnic and Tourist Arts.* Nelson Graburn, ed. Berkeley: University of California Press, 1976.

Caillié, Réné. *Travels Through Central Africa to Timbuctoo* (1827-1828). *2* vol. London: Frank Cass & Co., 1968.

Carroll, K. F. Three Generations of Yoruba Carvers. Ibadan 12:21-24, 1961.

Clamens, G. Une Phase de l'initiation à un poro forgeron sénoufo. *Notes Africaines* 65:9-14, 1955.

Clapperton, Hugh. *Travels and Discoveries in Northern and Central Africa.* London: John Murray, 1826.

Clignet, Remi. Urbanization and Family Structure in the Ivory Coast. *Comparative Studies in Society and History* 8:4:385-401, 1966.

Cole, Herbert M. Ibo Art and Authority. In *African Art and Leadership.* Douglas Fraser and Herbert M. Cole, eds. Madison: University of Wisconsin Press, 1972.

_____. The History of Ibo *Mbari* Houses—Facts and Theories. In *African Images: Essays in African Iconology.* Daniel F. McCall and Edna G. Bay, eds. New York: Africana Publishing Co., 1975.

Collieaux, M. L'Histoire de l'Ancien Royaume de Kénédougou. *Bulletin du Comité d'Etudes Historiques et Scientifiques* 7:128-181, 1924.

Colson, Elizabeth. Plateau Tongo. In *Matrilineal Kinship.* David M. Schneider and Kathleen Gough, eds. Berkeley: University of California Press, 1962.

Cook, Scott. Price and Output Variability in a Peasant-Artisan Stoneworking Industry in Oaxaca, Mexico. *American Anthropologist* 72:776-801, 1970.

Cordwell, Justine M. African Art. In *Continuity and Change in African Cultures.* William R. Bascom and Melville J. Herskovits, eds. Chicago: University of Chicago Press, 1970.

Crowley, Daniel J. Chokwe: Political Art in a Plebian Society. In *African Art and Leadership.* Douglas Fraser and Herbert M. Cole, eds. Madison: University of Wisconsin Press, 1972.

_____. Aesthetic Value and Professionalism in African Art: Three Cases from the Katanga Chokwe. In *The Traditional Artist in African Societies.* Warren d'Azevedo, ed. Bloomington: University of Indiana Press, 1973.

_____. Review of *Ethnic and Tourist Arts* (Nelson Graburn, ed.) *African Arts* 10:4:8, 1977.

d'Azevedo, Warren. *The Artist Archtype in Gola Culture.* Desert Research Institute Reprint #14. Reno: University of Nevada, 1970.

Delafosse, Maurice. Rapport du Cercle de Korhogo. ANCI 1EE79(2). October 20, 1908a.

_____. Le Peuple Siéna ou Sénoufo. *Revue des Etudes Ethnographiques et Sociologiques* 1:16-33, 79-92, 151-158, 242-275, 483-486; 2:1-23, 1908b.

_____. *Haut-Sénégal-Niger.* Paris: Emile Larose, 1912.

Dem, Tidiane. La Philosophie sénoufo. Paper presented at a Colloquium on Indigenous Cultures, Lycée Houphouët-Boigney. Typescript. Korhogo, c1974.

Durston, John W. Entrepreneurs in the Mexican Peasant Economy: Negative Implications for Development. Paper presented at the Seventieth Annual Meeting of the American Anthropological Association. New York, 1970.

Fagg, William B. Perspective from Africa: Summary of Proceedings. In *The Artist in Tribal Society.* Marian W. Smith, ed. New York: The Free Press, 1961.

_____. *African Sculpture from the Tara Collection.* Notre Dame, Indiana: Art Gallery of the University of Notre Dame, 1971.

Fernandez, James. Artistic Expression in Fang Culture. In *The Traditional Artist in African Societies.* Warren d'Azevedo, ed. Bloomington: University of Indiana Press, 1973.

Ferreol. Essai d'Histoire et d'Ethnographie sur Quelques Peoplades de la Subdivision de Banfora. *Bulletin du Comité d'Etudes Historiques et Scientifiques* 7:100-127, 1924.

Fiches Signalétiques des Chefs Indigènes. ANCI 2EE8(13), 1918-1928.

Forde, Daryll, ed. *Efik Traders of Old Calabar.* London: International, 1968.

_____ and Scott, Richenda. *The Native Economies of Nigeria.* London: Faber and Faber, 1946.

Fortes, Meyer. *The Web of Kinship among the Tallensi.* London: Oxford University Press, 1949.

_____. Kinship and Marriage among the Ashanti. In *African Systems of Kinship and Marriage.* A. R. Radcliffe-Brown and Daryll Forde, eds. London: Oxford University Press, 1967.

Foster, George. *Traditional Cultures: and the Impact of Technological Change.* New York: Harper and Row, 1962.

_____. *Tzintzuntzan.* Boston: Little, Brown & Co., 1967.

Franz, Mary Louise. Traditional Masks and Figures of the Makonde. *African Arts* 3:1:42-45, 1969.

Furst, Peter T. *Myth in Art: A Huichol Depicts His Reality.* Los Angeles: Latin American Center, University of California, 1968/1969.

Gardi, René. *African Crafts and Craftsmen.* New York: Van Nostrand Reinhold Co., 1969.

149

_____. *Indigenous African Architecture*. New York: Van Nostrand Reinhold Co., 1973.

Gill, Robert R. Ceramic Arts and Acculturation at Laguna. In *Ethnic and Tourist Arts*. Nelson Graburn, ed. Berkeley: University of California Press, 1976.

Glaze, Anita. Personal Communication, 1972, 1977.

_____. Woman Power and Art in a Senufo Village. *African Arts* 8:3:24ff, 1975.

_____. *Art and Death in a Senufo Village (Kufulo/Fodonon Region)*. Ann Arbor: University Microfilms International, 1976.

Goldwater, Robert. *Senufo Art*. New York: Museum of Primitive Art, 1964.

Gough, Kathleen. The Modern Distribution of Matrilineal Descent Groups. In *Matrilineal Kinship*. David M. Schneider and Kathleen Gough, eds. Berkeley: University of California Press, 1962.

Graburn, Nelson H. H. Art as a Mediating Influence in Acculturation Processes. Paper presented at the Sixty-Ninth Annual Meeting of the American Anthropological Association. New Orleans, 1969.

_____. Eskimo Art: The Eastern Canadian Arctic. In *Ethnic and Tourist Arts*. Nelson Graburn, ed. Berkeley: University of California Press, 1976a.

_____. Introduction. In *Ethnic and Tourist Arts*. Nelson Graburn, ed. Berkeley: University of California Press, 1976b.

Griaule, Marcel and Dieterlen, Germaine. The Dogon. In *African Worlds*. Daryll Forde, ed. London: Oxford University Press, 1970.

Hammond, Peter B. Economic Change and Mossi Acculturation. In *Continuity and Change in African Cultures*. William R. Bascom and Melville J. Herskovits, eds. Chicago: University of Chicago Press, 1970.

Herskovits, Melville, J. *The Human Factor in Changing Africa*. New York: Vintage Books, 1967.

Himmelheber, Hans. *Negerkunst und Negerkunstler*. Brauschwerg: Vlinkhardt and Biermann, 1960.

_____. Personality and Technique of African Sculptors. In *Technique and Personality*. New York: Museum of Primitive Art, 1963.

_____. Gold-Plated Objects of Baule Notables. In *African Art and Leadership*. Douglas Fraser and Herbert M. Cole, eds. Madison: University of Wisconsin, 1972.

_____. Eine unafrikanische gestaltungstendenz in neu-afrikanischer bildender Kunst. *Zeitschrift fuer Ethnologie* 99:220-223, 1975.

Hodder, B. W. and Ukwu, U. I. *Markets in West Africa*. Ibadan: Ibadan University Press, 1969.

Holas, B. *Cultures materielles de la Côte d'Ivoire*. Paris, 1960.

_____. *Les Sénoufo*. Paris: Presses Universitaires de France, 1966.

_____. *Sculpture Ivorienne*. Abidjan, 1969.

Jamin, Jean. La Nébuleuse du Koulo Tyolo (Assai de rapport de state et d'enquête en pays Sénoufo). Typescript. Abidjan: Office de la Research Scientifique et d'Outre Mer, 1973.

Kent, Kate Peck. Pueblo and Navajo Weaving Traditions and the Western World. In *Ethnic and Tourist Arts*. Nelson Graburn, ed. Berkeley: University of California Press, 1976.

Kientz, Albert. Personal Communication, 1975.

Ki-Zerbo, Joseph. *Histoire de l'Afrique Noire*. Paris: Librairie Hatier, 1972.

Knops, P. l'Artisan Sénoufo dans son cadre Ouest-Africain. *Société Royal Belge d'Anthropologie et de Préhistoire* 70:83-111, 1959.

Koffi. De Quelques Aspects Historique et Coutumiers des Sénoufos des Régions de Korhogo et Boundiali. Typescript. Korhogo:El Nid [private orphanage], c1966.

Lathrap, Donald. Shipibo Tourist Art. In *Ethnic and Tourist Arts*. Nelson Graburn, ed. Berkeley: University of California Press, 1976.

Laye, Camara. *The African Child*. New York: Collins Fontana Books, 1954.

Lem, F. H. Au sujet d'une statuette Sénoufo. *Bulletin de l'Institut Fondamental d'Afrique Noire* 4:4:175-181, 1941.

Lloyd, P. C. Craft Organization in Yoruba Towns. In *Social Change: The Colonial Situation*. Immanuel Wallerstein, ed. New York: John Wiley & Sons, 1966.

Low, Setha M. Contemporary Ainu Wood and Stone Carving. In *Ethnic and Tourist Arts*. Nelson Graburn, ed. Berkeley: University of California Press, 1976.

Maduro, Renaldo. The Brahmin Painters of Nathdwara, Rajasthan. In *Ethnic and Tourist Arts*. Nelson Graburn, ed. Berkeley: University of California Press, 1976.

Maesen, A. Le Sculpteur dans la vie sociale chez les Sénoufo de la Côte d'Ivoire. *International Congress of Anthropological and Ethnological Sciences*. Compte-Rendu (Tervuren 1960), 1948.

May, R. J. Tourism and the Artifact Industry in Papua New Guinea. Paper presented at the Workshop on the Impact on Pacific Island Countries of the Development of Tourism. Hawaii: East-West Center, 1974.

Messenger, John C. The Role of the Carver in Anang Society. In *The Traditional Artist in African Society*. Warren d'Azevedo, ed. Bloomington: University of Indiana Press, 1973.

Ministère du Plan. *Esquisse de Structuration du Milieu Rural*. 2 vols. Republique de la Côte d'Ivoire. Département de Boundiali and Département de Korhogo, 1973.

Museum of Primitive Art. *African Sculpture from the Collection of Jay C. Less*. Catalogue. New York, 1964.

Nadel, S. F. *A Black Byzantium*. London: Oxford University Press, 1969.

Nash, Manning. The Social Context of Economic Choice in a Small Society. In *Tribal and Peasant Economics*. George Dalton, ed. Garden City: The Natural History Press, 1967.

Neaher, Nancy. Igbo Metalsmiths among the Southern Edo. *African Arts* 9:4:46-49, 1975.

Niane, D. T. *Sundiata: An Epic of Old Mali*. London: Longman Group, Ltd., 1970.

l'Office Nationale de l'Artisanat d'Art et le Ministère d'Etat Chargé du Tourisme. Catalogue. Abidjan, c1973.

Person, Yves. *Samori: Une Révolution Dyula*. Vols. I and II. Dakar: l'Institut Fondamental d'Afrique Noire, 1970.

_____. Guinea-Samori. In *West African Resistance*. Michael Crowder, ed. London: Hutchinson, 1971.

_____. Oral Traditions and Chronology. In *French Perspectives in African Studies*. Pierre Alexandre, ed. London: Oxford University Press, 1973a.

_____. Du Soudan nigerien a l'Atlantique. In *Histoire Générale de l'Afrique Noire de Madagascar et des Archipels*. Humbert Déschamps, ed. Paris: Presses Universitaires de France. Vol. II:Tome I, 1973b.

Post du Segoumo. Letter to the Chef de Cercle de Boundiali. ANCI 1EE93(1), May 1914.

Rapport. ANCI 1EE93(1), 1928.

Rapport annuel sur le travail. ANCI 1441(XVIII-30-54), 1938.

Rapport Mensuels. ANCI 1EE109(1/5), 1906.

Rapport des Tournées. ANCI 1EE109(1/7), July 1909.

Raum, E. F. Artist, Art Patron and Art Critic in Changing Africa. *Fort Hare Papers* 3:3-13, 1966.

Richter, Dolores. The Tourist Art Market as a Factor in Social Change. *Annals of Tourism Research* 5:3:323-338, 1978.

_____. Senufo Mask Classification. *African Arts* 12:3:66-73, 1979.

_____. Further Considerations of Caste in West Africa: The Senufo. *Africa*, in press.

Ritter, E. A. *Shaka Zulu*. New York: New American Library, 1973.

Rubins, Arnold. *The Sculptor's Eye*. Washington, D.C.: Museum of African Art, 1976.

Ryerson, Scott H. Seri Ironwood Carvings: An Economic View. In *Ethnic and Tourist Arts*. Nelson Graburn, ed. Berkeley: University of California Press, 1976.

Schädler, Karl-Ferdinand. Impact of Tourism on Traditional Arts and Crafts and the Values Associated with Them in Some African Counties South of the Sahara. Paper presented at the Joint UNESCO/IBRD Seminar on the Social and Cultural Impacts of Tourism. Washington, D.C., December 8-10, 1976.

Schapera, I. Economic Changes in South African Native Life. In *Tribal and Peasant Economics*. George Dalton, ed. Garden City: The Natural History Press, 1967.

Schwab, W. B. Continuity and Change in the Yoruba Lineage System. In *Black Africa: Its People and Their Cultures Today*. John Middleton, ed. London: The Macmillan Co., 1970.

Shack, William. Notes on Occupational Castes among the Gurage of Southwest Ethiopa. *Man* 54:50-52, 1964.

Shore-Bos, Megchelina. Modern Makonde: A Discovery in East African Art. *African Arts* 3:1:46-51, 80-81, 1969.

Sieber, Roy. Kwahu Terracottas, Oral Traditions and Ghanaian History. In *African Art and Leadership*. Douglas Fraser and Herbert M. Cole, eds. Madison: University of Wisconsin Press, 1972.

Statistique administratif, ethnique et économique. ANCI 1EE109(1/7), October 20, 1908.

Stenning, Derrick J. *Savannah Nomads*. London: Oxford University Press, 1959.

Stout, J. A. *Modern Makonde Sculpture*. Moshi, Tanzania: Kibo Art Gallery Publications, 1966.

Stromberg, Gobi. The Amate Bark-Paper Painting of Xalitla. In *Ethnic and Tourist Arts*. Nelson Graburn, ed. Berkeley: University of California Press, 1976.

Thoret, J. C. *l'Artisanat dans la région de Dabakala*. l'Institut d'Ethnosociologie. Abidjan: l'Université d'Abidjan, 1971.

Tibor, Bodrigi. *Art in Africa*. New York: McGraw-Hill, 1968.

Turner, V. W. *Schism and Continuity in an African Society*. Manchester: Manchester University Press, 1957.

Vaughan, Jr., James H. Caste Systems in the Western Sudan. In *Social Stratification in Africa*. A. Tuden and L. Plotnicov, eds. New York: The Free Press, 1970.

_____. əngkyagu as Artists in Marghi Society. In *The Traditional Artist in African Societies*. Warren d'Azevedo, ed. Bloomington: University of Indiana Press, 1973.

von Sydow, Eckart. African Sculpture. *Africa* 1:210-241, 1928.

Watson, William. *Tribal Cohesion in a Money Economy*. New York: The Humanities Press, 1964.

Welmers, William E. Notes on Two Languages of the Senufo Group. I. Senari. *Language* 26:126-146, 1950a.

_____. Notes on Two Languages of the Senufo Group. II. Sup'ide. *Language* 26:494-531, 1950b.

_____. *Report on Senufo Dialect Studies*. Korhogo: Mission Baptiste, 1957.

Williams, Nancy. Australian Aboriginal Art at Yirrkala: Introduction and Development of Marketing. In *Ethnic and Tourist Arts*. Nelson Graburn, ed. Berkeley: University of California Press, 1976.

World Bank. Current Economic Situation. Unpublished Report, 1972.

World Mark Encyclopedia of the Nations. "Africa." Vol. 2. New York: John Wiley & Sons, 1976.

Zemp, Hugo. "The Music of the Senufo." Edited for the International Music Council by the International Institute for Comparative Music Studies and Documentation. New York: UNESCO. Baron Reiter Musicaphon BM30L2308, c1965.

INDEX

Abidjan 45, 53, 56, 89, 112, 115, 127, 145
Age grades, see Poro
Agnates 30, 41, 43, 58, 92
Agnibilikrou 14
Ancestors 1, 14, 21, 47, 49, 118, 141; village-of-the-dead 49, 85
Antique art 10, 108-109, 114, 115, 118, 134-135
Antique art market 2, 108-109; theft for 108-109, 134-135
Apprentices 32, 33, 50, 64-65, 66, 67-68, 85, 99, 103, 120
Art, see Antique art; commercial fine 10, 68; critics 3, 67-69, 70-71, 125, 127, 145; and economics 2-3, 5; see Mass-production; and religion 1-3; souvenir 10, 66; see Tourist art; see Traditional art
Art dealers 10, 18, 36, 70-71, 72, 86, 88, 92, 102, 109, 112, 118, 135; competition between 111; European 65, 70, 110; Hausa 65, 70, 111, 112-113, 126, 127, 134-135; Ivorian government 112-113, 127; Kulebele 52-53, 55, 58-59, 67, 70, 88, 92, 108-112, 114, 115-116, 118, 121, 124, 126-127; Senegalese 65, 70, 111, 112-113, 126-127
Artisan groups ("castes") 11-15, 18, 136; Cedumbele 15; Dalebele 14, 49; Fa7abele 15; see Fonombele; see Jelebele; see Kpeembele; see Kulebele; Logon 13; Lorho 13; Numu 14; Shagibele 15; Sindumbele 15
Artisans 15; African 1-4, 5, 6; Anang 2; Bangway 2, 129; Baule 3; see Blacksmiths; Eskimo 6; Fang 69; Fuga 93; Gola 68-69; goldsmiths 15, 94; gunsmiths 15; Ibo 3; see Jelebele; Kran 2, 3; Kwahu 69; Laguna potters 7, 15, 69; Lobi 7; Logon 13; Lorho 13, 130; Makonde 6, Nigerian 2, 138; Nupe 7; potters 129, 143; Seri 6, 7; Shipibo-Conibo 129; status of 12-13, 70, 93, 136; supernatural powers of 52-53, 58, 93-94, 103, 134, 144; weavers 13, 15, 112, 129; Xatitlan 6; Yirrkala 6, 129
Arts/crafts, bark painting 6, 7, 129; baskets 4, 14; beads 4; brass 4, 5, 13, 15, 106; charms 4, 5, 15; *cire perdue* 13, 15; cloth dying 4; gold 13, 15; iron 4, 13, 106; ivory 13; jewelry 4, 5, 13, 15, 143; leather 4, 13, 15, 143; mats 4, 14; pottery 4, 13, 15, 143; stone 13; weaving 4, 15, 106, 143; woodcarving 3, 4, 6, 13-15, 61-69, 70-71, 106
Ateliers, government 112, 121, 138
Art market, see Antique art market; see Tourist art market; see Traditional art market
Avunculocality, see Residence patterns

Dabakaha 16, 19; Kulebele 17, 19, 77, 81, 82, 83; Poro 40, 144
Dakar 112
Dalir xv, 8, 14, 131
Dancers 48-49, 51-52, 58, 95, 107
Dancing 48-49, 51-52, 125; competition 49, 51-52; see Poro
Danebolo 16, 17, 18, 19, 87; and Djemtana 56; and Korhogo 53-57; Kulebele 17, 18, 19, 81; migration 18, 53-54; political organization 53-57; Poro 49, 53-57, 132, 143; poverty 55-56, 144; and Sumo 56; and tourist art market 54-56
Death 18, 53, 54, 58, 94, 100, 139
Delafosse, M. 8-9
Development 18, 143; building codes 18, 34-37, 114, 124, 145; Office National de l'Artisanat d'Art de Côte d'Ivoire 112-113; redistribution of land 18, 92, 124, 131-132
Dikodougou 11, 14, 15, 16, 22, 61, 67, 90, 114, 135, 145
Divination 53; Kafigelejo 57-58
Diviners 84
Divorce 61
Djemtana 16, 19, 87, 134; and Danebolo 56; and Korhogo 52, 55; Kulebele 17, 19, 81; and Nafoun 52; Poro 49, 50, 52
Drums 10, 47, 48, 65, 101, 113, 132, 133
Dyula 8, 9, 12, 14, 15, 18, 19, 20, 36, 40, 50-51, 53, 65, 97, 100, 112, 121, 130; chiefs 130; definition of 130; kinship terms 22, 26

Economic, exploitation 52-53, 54, 55, 56, 70, 88, 123, 127; sanctions 52, 54, 55-56
Economy, cash 5, 6; subsistence 5, 124, 125
Education, western 5, 115, 116
Elders 18, 31-32, 37, 44, 45, 56, 57, 84, 94-95, 97, 103, 112, 120, 122, 135, 137, 144; Poro 44, 47-49, 51, 54, 57
Endogamy 13, 26, 27, 28, 96
Esthetics 1, 6-7, 67-69, 70-71, 125-126, 127-129, 135, 144, 145
Ethnic quarters 18-20, 44, 131
Ethnic relationships 18-20, 28-29, 37, 44-46, 50-51, 56, 61, 65, 84-85, 86, 89, 90, 93, 94-104, 117-118, 130, 133, 135, 136, 137
Exogamy 13, 21, 26-27, 28-29, 41, 45, 84, 95-97

Farmers, relationships with Kulebele 17, 28, 37, 44, 65, 90, 94-104, 110, 114; see *Senambele*
Farming 12-13, 37, 47-48, 50, 90; cash-crop 88, 90, 114; Kulebele 37, 39-40, 45, 47, 48, 61, 62, 66, 84, 88, 106-107, 136; land use-rights 20, 37, 86, 88, 90, 91; subsistence 88, 91, 114
Fijembele 9, 12-15, 20, 44-46, 100, 130, 141
Fodombele 9

Kacolo, see Residence units

Kafigelejo 57, 94-96, 97-98, 135; divination 57-58; negative supernatural sanctions 57-58, 96, 97-98, 100, 101, 102-103, 137; protection 58, 95-96, 97; sacrifice to 94-95, 136, 140

Kano, Nigeria 4

Kanono 16, 17, 18, 19, 89, 130; and Korhogo 55; Kulebele 17-18, 19, 61, 81; Poro 49

Kassembele 8

Kenedougou, kingdom of 8, 119

Kinship 21-28; changes in terms 22; Dyula influence 22-23; terms 22-26, 120, 130

Koko, see Quartier Koko

Kolia 16, 17, 19, 87, 88, 114, 130, 131, 132, 144; and Korhogo 55; Kulebele 17, 19, 28, 44, 53, 76, 81, 82, 83, 114-115, 124, 131, 132; Poro 49, 124, 132

Kolocelo 68, 99, 105

Kong 50-51

Korhogo 8, 9, 12, 15, 16, 17, 18, 19, 20, 32, 38, 40, 44, 45-46, 56, 57, 87-88, 89, 90, 91, 102, 105, 110, 111, 112, 113-115, 118, 120, 121, 122, 123, 130, 132, 133, 134, 137, 138, 139, 144; and Bolpe 55; and Danebolo 53-57; and Djemtana 55; *kafu* 32, 44, 51-57, 58-59, 63, 95, 110, 134, 145; and Kanono 55; and Kolia 55; Kulebele 17, 18, 19, 20, 32, 37-38, 40, 44, 61, 67, 68, 81, 88-89, 110-116, 143; and Nafoun 51-53; Muslims 57-59, 121; politics 52-59, 120, 121; Poro 49, 50, 51-55, 56, 57-59, 95, 132, 143; and Sumo 55; tourist art market 52-53, 54-55; women in 40-41

Kouto 16, 17, 19, 87, 130; Kulebele 17, 19, 81; Poro 49

Kpatobele 9

Kpeembele 9, 13, 15, 19, 130, 143

Kposulugo 16, 19, 22, 89; Kulebele 17, 19, 22, 81; Poro 49

Kufulo 9, 134, 135

Kufuru 8

Kulebele 13, 14, 15, 19; see Art dealers; Dalebele 14; eastern xv, 14, 22-24, 26-28, 29, 41, 66, 81, 88-89, 99, 115, 131, 139; relationships with non-Kulebele 18-20, 28, 29, 37, 44, 45, 50-51, 56, 61, 84-85, 86, 89, 90, 93, 94-104, 106, 107-108, 109, 111, 121, 123, 133, 134-135, 136; rural 37, 40, 116; villages 17-19, 20, 86-87, 101; western 14, 22-23, 25, 26-28, 29, 41, 67, 81, 84, 87, 88-89, 114-115, 131

Labor 44, 103, 123; see Apprentices; see Bride service; children's 28, 37, 39, 62, 107, 111; division of 37-41, 106-107; income generating (men's) 37, 107, 109-110; income generating (women's) 38-41, 100; forced 83, 98, 109, 136; men's 37, 61; see Poro; women's 39-41, 88, 91, 99, 107; see Work

Land 121; distribution 37; government redistribution 18, 34-35, 92; scarcity of 37, 39, 40, 41, 88, 123; use-rights 20, 37, 86, 88, 90, 91, 118

Laws, building codes 18, 34-37, 92; inheritance 33-34
Levirate 41
Livestock 33, 37, 38, 44, 45, 47, 54, 55, 61, 84, 85, 86, 97, 98, 99, 102, 106, 108, 110, 115, 118, 123, 136, 145; cattle 12, 52, 79, 106-107, 114, 115, 138; horses 106, 116; investment in 84, 85, 106-107, 114, 115, 116
Luck 99; bad 99, 105; good 76

Mali 11, 15, 16, 17, 81, 106
Mande 8, 9, 12, 13, 14, 15
Marketing 106, 118, 143; see Antique art; see Tourist art; see Traditional art; women's 38-40, 140
Marriage 26-30, 85-86, 103, 130, 131; changes in patterns 26, 41, 120, 121, 137, 138; endogamous 13, 26-28; exchange 28; exogamous 13, 26-28, 41, 45, 84, 95-97; half-sibling 28, 131; and political alliance 28, 29
Masks 13, 14, 136; brass 5, 15; face 4, 65, 125, 143, 144; helmet 4, 65, 77, 78, 101, 125, 140, 144-145; tourist 52, 55, 65-69, 70-71, 78, 80, 91, 100, 101, 102, 144, 145; traditional 45, 48, 51, 53, 57, 61, 66-67, 68, 71, 77, 101-102, 125, 144
Mass-production of art 3, 5, 70, 90, 110, 115, 126-127, 144, 145
Master carvers 62, 65, 66, 67, 68-69, 71, 72, 86, 106, 108, 126, 127, 144
Matrilineage 20, 131; see *Narigba7a*
Matrilineality 9, 21, 120-121
Mbengue 14, 16, 17
Meat 31, 37, 71, 84, 95, 122-123, 136, 139-140
Medical care 17, 19, 51, 113, 122-123, 139
Medicine 37, 84; indigenous 51, 56, 58, 137, 139; preventative 98
Menopause 30, 46, 133
Metamorphism 97-98
Middlemen 70, 108, 110-113, 143
Migration 7, 15, 17, 20, 40, 44-45, 50, 53, 55, 59, 61, 66, 67, 83-92, 102-103, 113, 117-118, 120, 124, 144; colonial 82-83, 110; precolonial 81-83, 87; rural 90-91, 92, 119; urban 40, 87, 89, 91-92, 110, 115, 123
Missionaries 90, 139
Modernization 1, 5, 88, 117, 122, 124, 125, 132; see Development
Money 19, 31, 33, 44, 47, 48-49, 54, 55, 56, 57, 84, 91, 103, 106, 108, 124, 132; cowries 29, 65, 84, 85, 86, 90, 100, 106-107, 108, 110, 114, 118, 136, 138; distribution of 47, 48, 49; francs 29, 65-66, 71, 90, 97, 100, 108, 109, 138; management of 39, 40, 54, 65-66, 84, 90-91, 98, 106-107
Monopoly, occupational 38, 65, 93, 97-104, 106, 114, 118
Mother's brother, see *Sheleo*
Motorbikes 48, 88, 89, 91, 110, 115, 119, 124
Musée d'Abidjan 53, 55, 56, 89, 136
Music 46, 56

44, 47-49, 50, 54, 55, 56; lodges 46-47, 49; masks 45, 48, 51, 53, 57, 67, 68, 101, 133, 134, 137; masqueraders 133-134, 137; music 46, 47, 48, 51; musical instruments 46, 47, 53, 108, 132-134; non-initiates 95, 102, 137, 140; organization 46-49; see Politics; recruitment for 50, 52-55, 56-57; see *Senambele;* see *Sinzang;* and women 102, 132, 133-134

Poverty 55-56, 85, 91, 124, 137, 139-140, 144

Préfecture 12, 130

Prestige 5, 91

Prostitutes 40-41

Public transportation 18, 89, 119, 125, 143

Quartier Koko 18, 67, 68, 113, 143, 144

Real estate 52, 59, 115; inheritance of 33-34; investment in 5, 113-114, 115, 116, 118; rural 108, 114, 116

Reciprocity 20, 31, 33

Religion, and art 2-3, 4; and artists 1, 125; and social change 4, 102-103, 120, 121

Rent 105, 114, 116

Rental property 5, 36, 106, 114, 115-116, 122, 145

Residence patterns 9, 18-20, 28, 29-37; avunculocal 28, 30, 31, 44; changes in 31-37, 92; children's 28, 30, 32; duolocal 9, 28-29; matrilocal 9; patrilocal 9, 29, 31-34, 43, 44; wives' 29-30, 34-36

Residence units 130; *gbagui* 31; *kacolo* 30-38, 39, 40, 43, 47-48, 53, 54, 92, 96, 122, 123, 131, 133, 141, 143

Risk-taking, minimizing 108, 114, 115, 116

Sacred grove, see *Sinzang*

Sacrifices 106; to Kafigelejo 94-95, 136, 140

Samori 12, 51, 81, 119, 130

San 14, 15, 16, 19, 22; Kulebele 17, 19, 22, 81, 130, 135; Poro 49

School 111, 113, 115

Secret society 1, 10, 15, 46, 129, 132, 144; see Poro; see Wambele

Segou, Mali 15, 16, 81

Senambele 9, 12-13, 17, 19, 20, 21, 28, 44-46, 48, 49, 50, 51, 117, 120-121, 122, 123, 132, 134-135, 137, 139, 140, 141; chiefs 17, 57, 86, 119, 120-121, 142; Poro 45, 49, 51, 55-56, 57, 58, 99, 100, 102, 106, 108, 119, 123, 132, 133, 134-135, 137, 138, 143; relations with Kulebele 17, 37, 123, 134-135; woodcarvers 13, 102-103, 120, 121, 123

Senari xv, 8, 9, 11, 14, 15, 22, 130

Senegalese 65, 70, 111, 112-113, 126-127

Senufo 6, 10, 11, 12-14, 15, 17, 18, 21, 28, 31, 44, 46, 47, 61, 65, 68, 69, 97, 112, 119, 127, 130, 134, 135, 137, 145; definition of 7-9

40-41, 123; occupations 13-15, 38-41, 83-84, 88, 91, 100; and Poro 102, 132, 133-134; wage labor 40

Wood for carving 63, 98-100; shortage of 89-90

Woodcarvers 13-14; see Apprentices; Anang 2, Bangway 2, 129; Baule 3; categories of 66, 67-69, 70, 71, 126, 127; Cedumbele 15, Dalebele 14, 49; Fang 71; see Fonombele; Fuga 93; Gola 68-69; hack 66, 67-68, 69, 70, 71, 126-127; Kran 2, 3; see Kulebele; Lobi 7; Makonde 6; see Master carvers; New Guinea 6; Nigeria 2; Seri 6, 7; specialized 51-62; see Supernatural powers; teenage 63, 66, 67-68, 136, 144

Work 37-41; attitudes towards 40, 105, 106

Work-groups 63-64

Woro 88

Zanguinasso 16, 19, 87; Kulebele 17, 19, 81; Poro 49

Zokenya 57

Zoomorphism 97-98